MITZIE WILSON
AND NICHOLA PALMER

BAKING AND BREAD

HAMLYN

Produced by New Leaf Productions

Photography by Mick Duff
Design by Jim Wire
Typeset by System Graphics
Series Editor: James M. Gibson

Published by The Hamlyn Publishing Group Limited,
Bridge House, 69 London Road,
Twickenham, Middlesex, England

First published 1987

Copyright © The Hamlyn Publishing Group Limited 1987

ISBN 0 600 327035

Printed in Hong Kong by Mandarin Offset

CONTENTS

INTRODUCTION

There is nothing quite like the satisfaction of baking your own bread and cakes. A cozy, warm kitchen and the lingering smell really make you think of the food Mum and Grandma used to make. But there is nothing old-fashioned about baking bread. It's healthy, delicious, economical and not as time consuming as you may think. Even if you're busy working all day, you can still knock up a loaf in between watching the television and cooking your supper — just right for tomorrow's breakfast. And if you use all the latest kitchen wizardry, mixers, microwaves, freezers and food processors, one batch of baking will set you up for a week or two.

Flours

A wide variety of flour is available in the shops. Choosing the right one for the type of baking you are doing will ensure the best possible results. Generally a recipe will state the type of flour to use, but if it doesn't, here is a guide to help you choose.

There are three basic categories of flour. They are defined by their rate of extraction, or the percentage of whole cleaned wheat grain that is present in the flour.

Wholemeal or wholewheat—100% extraction. The flour contains the whole wheat grain with nothing added and nothing taken away. Sometimes this flour is also called 'stoneground', which simply means that the wheat is ground between two stones instead of the modern steel roller mill process.

Brown—85% extraction. Lighter than wholemeal, this flour has the coarser part of the bran removed. Baking with wholemeal and brown flour gives a delicious nutty flavour, but gives a limited rise and closer texture than baking with white flour. Wholemeal and white flours can be mixed to achieve the rise and flavour preferred. Wholemeal flour is noted for its high dietary fibre content which is recommended for the healthy functioning of the digestive system. Brown and white flour contain less dietary fibre.

White—About 75% extraction. Most of the bran and wheatgerm is removed when the flour is milled. Look out for unbleached flour; it's now readily available in supermarkets.

Other flours readily available in supermarkets include:

Malted wheat—This brown flour with added grains of malted wheat gives a distinctive texture and nutty flavour as in Granary bread.

Rye—Used mainly in Continental breads, it has a slightly sour flavour, and lacks gluten so the loaves have a limited rise.

Types of flour also come with a variety of cooking characteristics.

Plain—Usually a white flour, but can be brown or wholemeal. It should be chosen when a raising agent is unnecessary, such as for shortcrust pastry, thickening sauces or pancakes. You can add a raising agent if desired.

Self raising—It can be white, brown or wholemeal and is simply plain flour to which raising agent has been added. It eliminates errors in measuring the exact quantity of raising agent required. It is used for cakes and puddings.

Soft—This contains a higher proportion of starch than strong flours. It produces a melt in the mouth texture and is ideal for biscuits, sponges and shortcrust pastry.

Strong—This has a higher protein content which when mixed with water forms plenty of high quality gluten. Gluten is very elastic and it is this which stretches and then sets on cooking to give a high volume and open texture. Therefore bread and other yeasted goods as well as puff and flaky pastry are best made with strong flour.

Bags of flour are now usually date stamped. This is particularly useful for wholemeal and brown flours where the fat in the wheat germ can go rancid in time, and for self raising flour where the raising agent can lose its efficiency. Wholemeal flour can be frozen if it is used infrequently. It remains free flow so that the quantity required can be easily removed. Allow it to come up to room temperature before using.

Yeasts

Yeast is a living plant which grows with warmth and food, that is, carbohydrates such as flour and sugar. As it grows, fermentation occurs giving off carbon dioxide gas. It is these bubbles of gas which stretch and raise the dough. Warmth helps speed the process, but too much heat kills the yeasts. Obviously, when you bake the dough in a hot oven, the yeast is killed, but this can also happen if the yeast is added to liquid which is too hot.

Fresh yeast is available from some bakers and health food shops. Buy it by the ounce. It should be a firm but crumbly texture with a fresh, clean yeasty smell. It should not be dry at the edges. Store it in the refrigerator loosely wrapped in cling film for up to three or four days.

To use fresh yeast, crumble the yeast onto the measured quantity of hand hot liquid and stir until blended. Add to the dry ingredients as stated in the recipe. It can be frozen. Cut into 15-g/½-oz portions, wrap individually in foil and place in a polythene bag. Store for up to six weeks. On thawing the yeast will soften; therefore it is easier to add the frozen yeast to the quantity of liquid stated in the recipe.

Dried yeast is available in small sachets or larger tins from supermarkets and chemists. It is best to buy the smaller sachets, unless you make bread regularly, because once opened dried yeast will deteriorate and should be used within 4 months.

To use dried yeast, dissolve 1 teaspoon of sugar in 125 ml/¼ pint hand-hot liquid taken from the quantity given in the recipe. Sprinkle the dried yeast on top, stir and leave for 10 to 15 minutes until frothy. If after this time the yeast has not frothed, the yeast is inactive and should be thrown away. Add the yeast liquid to the dry ingredients with the remaining liquid as stated in the recipe. Dried yeast is so concentrated that 15 g/½ oz will do the work of 25 g/1 oz fresh yeast.

Instant yeast is sold in foil sachets sometimes called fast action or easy blend yeast. It is a mixture of dried yeast and bread improvers, which give a large volume and light texture to bread doughs. The dough takes less time to rise.

To use instant yeast, simply stir the instant yeast into the dry ingredients. Do not reconstitute. A 15-g/½-oz sachet will do the work of 25 g/1 oz of fresh yeast.

Grains and seeds

The addition of grains and seeds, either worked into the dough or used as a topping, adds variety in both flavour and texture.

Cracked wheat, a coarsely ground wholewheat, adds crunch and a nutty flavour when worked into the dough and gives a rustic finish when sprinkled over brown and wholemeal breads.

Buckwheat, a triangular seed, can be worked into brown and wholemeal dough on its own or with other grains.

Bran has little flavour and is used mainly for its texture and high dietary fibre content.

Wheat germ is the part of the wheat grain containing a high proportion of protein, minerals and vitamins. Add flakes to enrich all baking.

Oats are available in a variety of forms, as oatmeal, rolled oats and as whole grain. They are used in many forms of baking including bread, cakes, scones and biscuits.

Rye meal is coarser than rye flour and gives a crunchy loaf.

Poppy seeds give colour, flavour and texture. They are usually used for white bread.

Sesame seeds make good crunchy topping for bread and rolls.

Caraway seeds are aromatic and characteristic of German and Scandinavian cooking. They are often added to rye breads.

Cumin seeds look similar to caraway seeds and also have a powerful aromatic flavour. They are used in many Indian, Middle Eastern and Moroccan dishes.

Sunflower seeds give a good nutty flavour and add extra protein.

Terms used in bread-making

Mixing—add the liquid to the dry ingredients in one go and mix with a wooden spoon or with one hand until a dough is formed. If using a mixer with a dough hook, mix on the slowest speed until the mixture forms a dough.

Kneading—to knead, turn the dough onto a lightly floured work surface. Fold the dough in half towards you, then push down with the palms and heels of your hands and away from you. Give the dough a quarter turn and repeat the folding and pushing action developing a rocking rhythm. This action develops the gluten in the dough to give a high volume loaf. At first the dough will be soft and sticky, but as the gluten develops, the dough will become smooth, elastic and no longer sticky. There is a temptation initially to add more flour to the sticky dough, but avoid this as it will make the finished loaf hard and tough. Kneading by hand is hard work, it takes about 5 minutes for a wholemeal or brown dough and 10 minutes for a white dough, but it is a good way to get rid of pent up anger and frustrations! To knead in an electric mixer with a dough hook, increase the speed a little after the dough is formed,

kneading will take about half the time of hand kneading.

Rising—takes place after the dough is kneaded. It is left to rise to double its original volume. The dough must be covered to prevent a hard skin from forming. The easiest way is to place the dough in a lightly oiled polythene bag, large enough to allow the dough to rise. Alternatively place the dough in a lightly oiled bowl and cover with cling film or a lid, again allowing sufficient space for the dough to rise. The temperature at which the dough is left to rise will affect the time it takes. A warm place is obviously the quickest, and the slowest is in the refrigerator overnight. If leaving the dough overnight, use a little less yeast when making up the dough. A microwave can be used for raising dough if it is necessary to speed the process up. Use the lowest setting, and follow manufacturer's instructions for timings.

Knocking back—punch the risen dough to deflate it, then knead until firm. This distributes the air bubbles in the dough to ensure a more even texture. Large bubbles of gas would make large holes in the finished bread.

Proving—after shaping, the dough is left to rise again until double in size, light and puffy. It must be covered as for the first rising.

Making bread in a food processor

It is possible to make bread in a food processor, although you may be restricted on the quantity of dough depending on the size of the food processor bowl. It is best to follow manufacturer's instructions for mixing and kneading times.

Freezing bread and rolls

Generally, bread freezes very well. Crusty loaves have a limited life in the freezer as the crust tends to flake off after about one week. To freeze bread, cool after baking; then wrap in a polythene bag and seal.

Thaw at room temperature for 3-6 hours, depending on the size of the loaf, or wrap the frozen loaf in foil and heat in a moderately hot oven (200°C, 400°F, gas 6) for 30-45 minutes. To thaw bread in a microwave, unwrap and cook on defrost for 2-8 minutes, depending on the quantity of bread and the power of the microwave. Always under-estimate timings; overcooking will give a hard loaf.

To bring back the crispness to a crusty loaf, refresh in a hot oven (220°C, 425°F, gas 7) for 10 minutes.

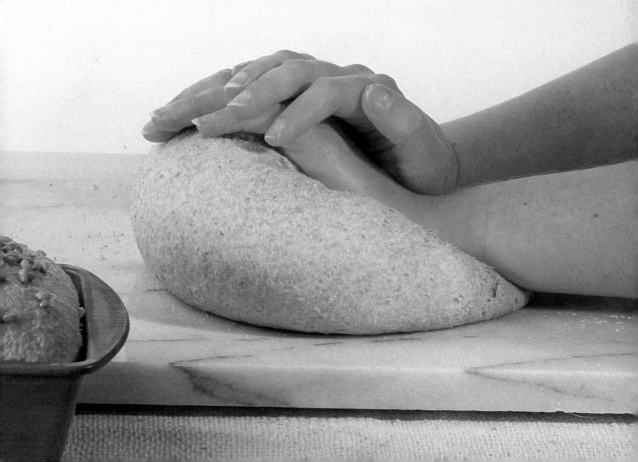

BASIC BREADS

BASIC WHITE BREAD

Makes one large loaf or two small loaves

**1½ teaspoons dried yeast and 1 teaspoon sugar
   or 15 g/½ oz fresh yeast**
450 ml/¾ pint hand-hot water
675 g/1½ lb strong white flour
2 teaspoons salt
15 g/½ oz lard
1 tablespoon milk to glaze

If using dried yeast, dissolve the sugar in 150 ml/
¼ pint hand-hot water taken from the 450 ml/¾
pint. Sprinkle the yeast onto the water and stir. Leave
for 10–15 minutes until frothy.

Sift the flour and salt together into a large bowl. If
possible place in a warm oven for 5 minutes. Rub in
the lard.

If using fresh yeast, crumble the yeast onto the
hand-hot water and stir until blended. Pour onto the
flour and mix to a soft dough. If using dried yeast,
add the yeast liquid with the remaining 300 ml/
½ pint water. Turn the dough out onto a lightly
floured work surface and knead until smooth and
elastic, about 10 minutes by hand or 5 minutes with
an electric dough hook. Place the dough in a lightly
oiled plastic bag and loosely seal. Leave in a warm
place to rise until doubled in size (about 1 hour).

Turn the dough onto a clean work surface and
knock back until smooth. Flatten the dough with
your hands. For a large loaf, shape the dough into an
oblong. Roll up like a Swiss roll, tuck the ends under
and drop into a greased 1-kg/2-lb loaf tin. For 2 small
loaves, cut the dough in half and shape as above and
place in two greased 450-g/1-lb loaf tins. Place back
in the polythene bag and loosely seal. Leave in a
warm place until the dough is again doubled in size or
until springy to the touch.

Remove the polythene bag, brush with milk and
bake in a preheated hot oven (230°C, 450°F, gas 8) for
30–40 minutes for the large loaf and 25–30 minutes for
the smaller loaves, until the crust is well browned and
beginning to shrink from the sides of the tin. Turn
out of the tin and tap the bottom of the loaf. If it
sounds hollow, the loaf is cooked. If not, return it to
the oven and cook for a few minutes more. Cool on
a rack.

ENRICHED WHITE BREAD

Makes 1 large loaf or 12 rolls

A batter is made first to start the yeast off, because the extra fat and egg in the recipe slow down the action of the yeast. This makes an excellent dough for soft rolls.

450 g/1 lb strong white flour
2 teaspoons dried yeast and 1 teaspoon sugar or
**   15 g/½ oz fresh yeast**
275 ml/9 fl oz hand-hot milk and water mixed
1 teaspoon salt
50 g/2 oz butter or margarine
1 egg, size 3, beaten

Sift 150 g/5 oz flour into a bowl. Stir the yeast into the milk. If using dried yeast, add the sugar and allow to stand for 5 minutes. Mix with the flour to make a batter and leave in a warm place until frothy, about 20 minutes.

Sift the remaining flour with the salt, into another mixing bowl and rub in the butter or margarine. Add the yeast batter and beaten egg and mix to form a soft dough. Turn onto a lightly floured work surface and knead until smooth and no longer sticky, about 10 minutes by hand or 5 minutes with an electric dough hook. Place in a lightly oiled polythene bag, loosely seal and leave in a warm place until doubled in size, about 1 hour.

Knock back the dough and shape into a loaf or rolls as required (see pages 12-15). After shaping, loosely cover and allow to rise again. Bake in a preheated hot oven (220°C, 425°F, gas 7) for 30-40 minutes for a loaf and 15-20 minutes for rolls. Cool on a rack.

MILK BREAD

Makes 1 large loaf, 2 small loaves or 18 rolls

This dough makes a soft loaf with a soft crust. The extra fat and the fat in the milk help to keep the bread moister for longer than the Basic White Bread. It is a good dough to use for making rolls.

2 teaspoons dried yeast and 1 teaspoon sugar or
**   15 g/½ oz fresh yeast**
450 ml/¾ pint hand-hot milk or milk and
**   water mixed**
675 g/1½ lb strong white flour
2 teaspoons salt
50 g/2 oz lard or margarine

If using dried yeast, dissolve the sugar in 150 ml/¼ pint hand-hot milk or milk and water mixed taken from the 450 ml/¾ pint. Sprinkle the yeast onto the water and stir. Leave for 10-15 minutes until frothy.

Sift the flour and salt together into a large bowl. If possible place in a warm oven for 5 minutes. Rub in the lard or margarine.

If using fresh yeast, crumble the yeast onto the hand-hot milk or milk and water mixed; stir until blended. Pour onto the flour and mix to a soft dough. If using dried yeast, add the yeast liquid with the remaining 300 ml/½ pint milk or milk and water mixed. Turn the dough out onto a lightly floured work surface and knead until smooth and elastic, about 10 minutes by hand or 5 minutes with an electric dough hook. Place the dough in a lightly oiled polythene bag and loosely seal. Leave in a warm place to rise until doubled in size, about 1 hour.

Turn the risen dough onto a clean work surface and knock back until smooth. Shape the dough into a loaf (see Basic White Bread page 8 and other shapes page 12) or rolls (see page 14). Glaze as required (see page 15). Loosely cover and allow to rise again until doubled in size or springy to the touch. Bake in a preheated hot oven (220°C, 425°F, gas 7) for 30-40 minutes for loaves and 15-20 minutes for rolls. Cool on a rack.

WHEAT GERM BREAD

Makes 1 large loaf or 2 small loaves

**2 teaspoons dried yeast and 1 teaspoon sugar or
    15 g/½ oz fresh yeast**
450 ml/¾ pint hand-hot water
550 g/1 lb 4 oz brown flour
50 g/2 oz bran
50 g/2 oz wheat germ
1 tablespoon soft dark brown sugar
2 teaspoons salt
25 g/1 oz lard or margarine
salt water glaze (see page 15)
**seeds, bran or wheat germ for sprinkling
    (optional)**

If using dried yeast, dissolve the sugar in 150 ml/¼ pint hand-hot water taken from the 450 ml/¾ pint. Sprinkle the yeast into the water and stir. Leave for 10-15 minutes until frothy.

Mix together the brown flour, bran, wheat germ, brown sugar and salt. Rub in the lard or margarine.

If using fresh yeast, crumble the yeast onto the hand hot water and stir until blended. Pour onto the flour and mix to a dough. If using dried yeast, add the yeast liquid with the remaining 300 ml/½ pint water. Turn the dough on to a lightly floured surface and knead until no longer sticky, about 10 minutes by hand or 5 minutes with an electric dough hook. Place the dough in a lightly oiled polythene bag and loosely seal. Leave in a warm place to rise until doubled in size, about 1¼ hours.

Turn the dough onto a clean work surface and knock back until firm again. Shape the dough (see Basic White Bread page 8 or other bread shapes page 12). Glaze with salt water and sprinkle with seeds, bran or wheat germ if liked. Cover loosely and leave in a warm place until doubled in size or until springy to the touch, about 45 minutes.

Bake in a preheated hot oven (220°C, 425°F, gas 7) for 30-40 minutes for a large loaf and 25-30 minutes for smaller loaves, until the bread sounds hollow when tapped on the bottom. Cool on a rack.

MIXED GRAIN BREAD

Makes 1 large loaf or 2 small loaves

The use of malt extract in brown bread dough adds a delicious flavour and slight sweetness. It is available from health food shops and chemists.

**1 tablespoon dried yeast and 1 teaspoon sugar
    or 25 g/1 oz fresh yeast**
400 ml/14 fl oz hand-hot water
350 g/12 oz wholemeal flour
225 g/8 oz strong white flour
2 teaspoons salt
25 g/1 oz lard
75 g/3 oz cracked wheat
25 g/1 oz buckwheat
25 g/1 oz whole oats
25 g/1 oz sunflower seeds
2 tablespoons malt extract
salt water glaze (see page 15)

If using dried yeast, dissolve the sugar in 150 ml/¼ pint hand-hot water taken from the 450 ml/¾ pint. Sprinkle the yeast onto the water and stir. Leave for 10-15 minutes until frothy.

Mix together the flours and salt in a bowl. Rub in the lard, then add the cracked wheat, buckwheat, oats and sunflower seeds. If using fresh yeast, crumble the yeast onto the hand-hot water, stir until blended. Add the malt, pour onto the flour and mix to a soft dough. If using dried yeast, add the yeast liquid with the remaining 300 ml/½ pint water and the malt. Turn the dough out onto a lightly floured surface and knead until elastic. Place the dough in a lightly oiled polythene bag and loosely seal. Leave in a warm place to rise until doubled in size, about 1 hour.

Turn the dough onto a clean work surface and knock back until smooth. Shape the dough (see Basic White Bread page 8 or other shapes page 12). Glaze with salt water and sprinkle with cracked wheat. Cover loosely and leave in a warm place until doubled in size or until springy to the touch, about 45 minutes. Bake in a preheated hot oven (220°C, 425°F, gas 7) for 30-40 minutes for a large loaf and 25-30 minutes for smaller loaves, until the bread sounds hollow when tapped on the bottom. Cool on a rack.

BASIC WHOLEMEAL BREAD

Makes one large loaf or two small loaves

Half wholemeal flour and half strong white flour can be used if preferred, or the wholemeal flour can be replaced with brown flour for a lighter loaf, or Granary flour for a malted flavour and crunchy texture. If using stoneground wholemeal flour, increase the fresh yeast to 25 g/l oz or the dried yeast to 3 teaspoons.

**2 teaspoons dried yeast and 1 teaspoon sugar or
   15 g/½ oz fresh yeast**
475 ml/16 fl oz hand-hot water
675 g/1½ lb wholemeal flour
2 teaspoons salt
1 teaspoon sugar
25 g/1 oz lard
salt water glaze (see page 15)
cracked wheat (optional)

If using dried yeast, dissolve the sugar in 150 ml/¼ pint hand-hot water taken from the 450 ml/¾ pint. Sprinkle the yeast onto the water and stir. Leave for 10-15 minutes until frothy.

Mix together the flour, salt and sugar. If possible place in a warm oven for 5 minutes. Rub in the lard.

If using fresh yeast, crumble the yeast onto the hand-hot water and stir until blended. Pour onto the flour and mix to a dough. If using dried yeast, add the yeast liquid with the remaining 300 ml/½ pint water. Turn the dough onto a lightly floured surface and knead until no longer sticky. Place the dough in a lightly oiled polythene bag and loosely seal. Leave in a warm place to rise until doubled in size, about 1¼ hours.

Turn the dough onto a clean work surface and knock back until firm again. Shape the dough (see Basic White Bread page 8 or other bread shapes page 12). Glaze with salt water and sprinkle with cracked wheat if liked. Cover loosely and leave in a warm place until doubled in size or until springy to the touch, about 45 minutes. Bake in a preheated hot oven (230°C, 450°F, gas 8) for 30-40 minutes for a large loaf and 25-30 minutes for smaller loaves, until the bread sounds hollow when tapped on the bottom. Cool on a rack.

BREAD SHAPES

Cob
Use ½ quantity Basic White, Wholemeal or Mixed Grain bread dough (see pages 8-11). Shape the dough into a round ball and flatten slightly. Place on a greased baking tray and using a sharp knife slash a cross on the top. Brush with milk or salted water. Cover loosely, leave to rise and bake in a preheated hot oven (230°C, 450°F, gas 8) for 30-35 minutes.

Farmhouse tin loaf
Follow the recipe for Basic White Bread (see page 8), but before leaving the loaf to rise in the tin, dust the top of the loaf with flour. When the dough has risen and just before baking, make a slit with a sharp knife along the length of the loaf.

Cottage loaf
Use ½ quantity Basic White or Milk Bread dough (see pages 8-9). Cut one-third off the piece of dough.

Shape each piece into a ball. Place the large ball on a greased baking tray and place the smaller one on the top. Fix the two pieces together by pushing a floured finger or handle of a wooden spoon through the centre of both pieces of dough. Dust the top of the loaf with flour. Cover loosely, allow to rise and bake in a preheated hot oven (230°C, 450°F, gas 8) for about 40 minutes.

Chequerboard
Use ½ quantity Basic White, Milk Bread, Wholemeal or Wheat Germ Bread dough (see pages 8-11). Shape the dough into a round ball, place on a greased baking tray and press to flatten. Brush with milk or salted water and, using a sharp knife, slash the surface to form a crisscross pattern. Cover loosely, allow to rise and bake in a preheated hot oven (230°C, 450°F, gas 8) for 25-30 minutes.

Bloomer

Use ½ quantity Basic White, Milk Bread, Wholemeal or Mixed Grain Bread dough (see pages 8-11). Form the dough into a sausage shape. Place on a greased baking tray and, using a sharp knife, make six diagonal slashes across the top of the loaf. Brush with beaten egg or milk. Loosely cover, allow to rise and bake in a preheated hot oven (230°C, 450°F, gas 8) for 30-35 minutes.

Scissor Snipped

Shape loaf or rolls as required and snip the top in a decorative pattern with a pair of scissors to make spikes. Cover loosely, allow to rise and bake as above.

Plait

Use ½ quantity Basic White, Milk Bread, Wholemeal or Wheat Germ Bread dough (see pages 8-11). Divide the dough into 3 equal pieces. Roll each piece into a sausage shape about 36 cm/14 inches long. Join the three pieces together at one end, plait loosely then pinch the ends together. Place on a greased baking tray, glaze and sprinkle with seeds if liked. Cover loosely and allow to rise for about 45 minutes. Bake in a preheated hot oven (220°C, 425°F, gas 7) for 30-35 minutes. Cool on a rack.

Crown

Use ½ quantity Milk Bread, Enriched White Bread, Mixed Grain or Wheat Germ Bread dough (see pages 8-10). Divide the dough into six equal pieces and roll each one into a round. Arrange five of the balls around the edge of a greased 18-cm/7-inch sandwich tin and place the remaining one in the centre. Glaze and sprinkle with poppy seeds or sesame seeds, if liked. Cover loosely and allow to rise for 30-35 minutes. Bake in a preheated hot oven (230°C, 450°F, gas 8) for 25-30 minutes. Cool on a rack.

BREAD ROLLS

Any of the white, brown or wholemeal bread recipes (see pages 8-11) can be used to make rolls. Bread dough made with 675 g/1½ lb flour will make approximately 18 rolls. For average-sized rolls use 50 g/2 oz bread dough. Unless otherwise stated in the shaping instructions, place rolls well apart on greased baking trays, cover loosely and allow to rise until doubled in size, about 35 minutes. Bake in a pre-heated hot oven (230°C, 450°F, gas 8) for 10-15 minutes. If using Milk Bread dough or Enriched White Bread dough bake in a preheated hot oven (220°C, 425°F, gas 7) for 15-20 minutes. Cool on a rack.

Dinner Rolls

Flatten the dough between the work surface and palm of the hand, rotate the hand using firm pressure at first, then ease off the pressure and cup your fingers round the dough to form a ball. With practice two rolls can be shaped at once, one under each hand.

Cottage

Cut off one-third of the dough. Shape each piece into a ball. Place the large ball on the baking sheet and place the smaller one on top. Flour your finger and push it right through the centre of both pieces of dough.

Knot

Roll the dough into a sausage 15 cm/6 inches long and tie into a simple knot.

Winkle

Roll the dough into a thin sausage about 25 cm/ 10 inches long, coil up tightly.

Two Strand Plait

Cut the dough in half and roll each piece into a sausage 20 cm/8 inches long. Place one strand on top of the other to make a cross. Take the two ends of the underneath strand and cross them over the top strand. Repeat this with the other strand, forming a tower. Repeat until the dough is used up; pinch the ends together and lay the plait on its side.

Bap
Shape the dough into a ball and flatten to 1-cm/½-inch thickness. Dredge with flour. When the rolls are baked, wrap in a tea towel to ensure a soft crust.

Hamburger Bun
Shape as for baps, glaze with beaten egg and sprinkle with sesame seeds. For serving with large burgers, use 75 g/3 oz dough.

Bridge Rolls
Use Milk Bread dough or Enriched White Bread dough (see page 9). Roll the dough into finger shapes. Place the rolls close together on the baking tray so that they join together on rising. Glaze with beaten egg.

Crescents
Roll out 350 g/12 oz dough into a circle about 1 cm/½ inch thick . Cut into 6 triangles. Roll up each triangle starting at the wide end and finishing at the point. Curl the ends round to form a crescent.

Cloverleaf
Divide the dough into three equal pieces. Roll each piece into a ball and place on a greased baking tray, touching, in the shape of a cloverleaf.

Glazes and finishes
Milk gives a slightly crusty shiny finish.

Salted water gives a crusty finish. Dissolve 2 teaspoons salt in 3 tablespoons hot water.

Egg gives a golden, soft finish. Use 1 beaten egg mixed with 1 tablespoon water or 1 egg yolk mixed with 2 teaspoons water.

Flour gives a soft finish. Lightly brush or dredge shaped dough with flour.

Sugar syrup gives a sweet finish. Dissolve 1 tablespoon sugar in 1 tablespoon hot water or milk.

BREADS OF THE WORLD

FRENCH BREAD
Makes 2 small loaves

It is difficult to reproduce true French bread, mainly because the flour is not available in this country.

2 teaspoons dried yeast and 1 teaspoon sugar or
** 15 g/½ oz fresh yeast**
300 ml/½ pint hand-hot water
25 mg tablet of ascorbic acid (vitamin c)
450 g/1 lb strong white flour
1 teaspoon salt
salt water glaze (see page 15)

If using dried yeast, sprinkle the yeast and sugar onto the water and stir. Leave for 10-15 minutes until frothy. If using fresh yeast, blend the yeast with the water. Crush the ascorbic acid tablet and stir into the yeast liquid.

Mix the flour and salt in a large mixing bowl. Add the yeast liquid all at once and mix to a soft dough. Turn the dough onto a lightly floured work surface and knead until the dough is firm and no longer sticky, about 10 minutes by hand or 4 minutes with an electric dough hook. Place the dough in a lightly oiled polythene bag and leave to rise in a warm place for about 20 minutes.

Divide the dough into two and roll each piece into an oblong about 41 cm/16 inches long. Roll up the dough like a Swiss roll and place on a lightly floured baking sheet. Make five diagonal slashes along the length of each loaf. Brush with salt water. Leave the dough uncovered in a warm place for about 1½ hours.

Bake in a preheated hot oven (220°C, 425°F, gas 7) with a tin of hot water in the bottom of the oven. After 15 minutes remove the tin of water and cook the loaves for a further 15-20 minutes until very crisp and brown. Cool on a rack. French bread is best eaten on the day of baking.

Variation

GARLIC BREAD
Beat together 100 g/4 oz softened butter, 1-2 crushed cloves of garlic, 2 tablespoons chopped fresh parsley, salt and freshly ground black pepper. Slice a cooked French loaf diagonally, but not right the way through. Spread the garlic butter over both sides of each slice and wrap the loaf in foil. Cook in a hot oven (220°C, 425°F, gas 7) for 20 minutes. Open up the foil for the last few minutes for a crisp crust. Serve warm.

CROISSANTS ✓

Makes 8

These take some time to make, but the end result is worth it. Try to work in a cool kitchen, open all the windows and leave yourself plenty of time to allow the dough to chill, or you will find the buttery layers melting and the dough difficult to handle.

25 g/1 oz fresh yeast or 15 g/½ oz dried yeast
  and 1 teaspoon sugar
150 ml/5 fl oz hand-hot milk
25 g/1 oz butter, melted but not hot
1 teaspoon salt
1 tablespoon sugar
350 g/12 oz strong white flour
100g/4 oz butter, chilled
egg and milk to glaze

If using dried yeast, dissolve 1 teaspoon sugar in 3 tablespoons of hand-hot water. Add the yeast and leave for 10-15 minutes until frothy. If using fresh yeast, blend it with 3 tablespoons of hand-hot water.

Pour the milk and butter into a large bowl; stir in the salt and sugar. Add the yeast liquid to the milk and stir well. Gradually stir in the flour using a wooden spoon; then gather the dough together with your hands.

Turn the dough out onto a lightly floured work surface and knead until smooth and elastic, about 10 minutes. Place the dough in a lightly oiled polythene bag and leave in a warm place to rise until doubled in size, or until springy to the touch, about 45 minutes.

Turn the dough out onto a clean work surface and knock back until smooth. Place the dough in a plastic bag and chill in the refrigerator for 30 minutes.

Roll the dough out on a lightly floured work surface to a rectangle about 13 cm by 38 cm/5 x 15 inch. Dot 100 g/4 oz butter evenly in rows across all the dough. Fold one-third of the dough into the centre; then fold the other third over that. Seal the three edges with the rolling pin, and press down lightly in the centre. Give the dough a half turn and roll it out to its original oblong size. Place on a plate and chill for 10-15 minutes. Fold the dough in three again. Seal with the rolling pin as before and roll out to an oblong again. Chill for 10-15 minutes. Repeat the rolling and chilling at least twice more.

Cut the dough in half. Roll out each half into a 15-cm/6-inch square. Cut into four triangles, using a razor sharp knife. Do not drag the knife or press the dough as this will compress the layers.

To shape the croissants, lightly roll the point of the triangle away from you with a rolling pin to elongate the shape. The tip can be thinner than the base of the croissant. Take each corner of the base between the thumb and forefinger and pull a little apart to stretch the dough. Then roll up the croissant from the base, tucking the tip under. Curve the rolls into a crescent shape and place on an oiled baking tray. Cover lightly with oiled food wrap. Leave in a warm place to rise for 20-30 minutes until doubled in size. Chill for 10 minutes to ensure that the butter is set. Prepare a hot oven (220°C, 425°F, gas 7). Brush croissants with a mixture of lightly beaten egg and milk, taking care not to brush over the flaky edges of the dough. Bake for 15 minutes until the croissants are golden and crisp. Eat as soon as possible.

BRIOCHE

Makes 12 small or 1 large brioche

This rich buttery dough is delicious for breakfast with apricot preserve, goes well with many savoury starters and is good toasted too.

15 g/½ oz fresh yeast or 1½ teaspoons dried
**   yeast and 1 teaspoon sugar**
1½ tablespoons warm water
225 g/8 oz strong plain flour
pinch of salt
1 tablespoon caster sugar
2 eggs, size 3, beaten
50 g/2 oz butter melted
beaten egg, to glaze

Blend the fresh yeast with the water, or sprinkle the dried yeast and sugar over the water and leave for 10-15 minutes until frothy. Sift the flour and salt into a large basin. Add the caster sugar. Stir the yeast liquid into the flour with the eggs and butter. Work into a soft dough. Turn the dough out onto a work surface lightly dusted with flour and knead for about 5 minutes. Place the dough inside an oiled polythene bag and allow to rise in a warm place for 1-1½ hours or until the dough is doubled in size and springy to the touch.

Lightly brush a 1-litre/2-pint fluted brioche mould (or 12 7.5-cm/3-inch individual fluted tins) with extra melted butter. Knock back the dough and knead it lightly. For the large brioche shape the dough into a ball and place in the mould. For individual brioche simply divide the dough into 12 pieces, shape each into a ball and place in the tins. Place the tins into a lightly oiled polythene bag and leave in a warm place until doubled in size, and risen almost to the top of the mould.

Brush the top lightly with beaten egg. Bake in a preheated hot oven (230°C, 450°F, gas 8) for 15-20 minutes for the large brioche, 10 minutes for the individual brioches, or until golden brown. Turn out and cool on a wire rack.

QUICK SAUSAGE BRIOCHE

Serves 8 to 12

Rich, moist, with a sausage surprise, this loaf is lovely for buffets and supper parties.

350 g/12 oz strong plain flour
½ teaspoon salt
40 g/1½ oz margarine
25 g/1 oz caster sugar
1 sachet fast action or easy blend yeast
8 tablespoons hand-hot milk
1 egg, size 2, beaten
250 g/8 oz traditional German sausage
beaten egg, to glaze
1 teapoon poppy seeds

Sift the flour and salt into a large mixing bowl. Add the margarine and rub in with the fingers until the mixture resembles breadcrumbs. Stir in the sugar and yeast and gradually add the milk. Add the eggs and beat to a soft dough. Turn onto a lightly floured work surface and knead until smooth, about 10 minutes. Roll the dough out to a rectangle large enough to wrap around the sausage. Skin the sausage and place along the centre of the dough. Brush the edges of the dough with water and wrap around the sausage pinching the edges to seal. Place seam side down on a greased baking tray. Place inside a large oiled polythene bag. Allow to rise until doubled in size (about 1 hour). Slash the top of the loaf at 2.5-cm/1-inch intervals, brush with beaten egg and sprinkle with poppy seeds. Bake in a moderately hot oven (200°C, 400°F, gas 6) for 15-20 minutes until golden. Cool on a wire rack. Serve hot, cold or even toasted.

BREAD STICKS
Makes 30

When baking bread, it is worth making some extra dough for bread sticks. They are delicious with dips and make a healthier alternative to crisps.

½ quantity Basic White or Wholemeal Bread dough (see pages 8 and 11)
milk or beaten egg white, to glaze
coarse salt, sesame seeds or poppy seeds

After the first rising, knock back the dough and return it to the oiled polythene bag. Break off a piece of dough about the size of a walnut and roll it into a strand about 30 cm/12 inches long. Place on a greased baking tray, repeat with remaining dough. Brush with milk or beaten egg white and sprinkle with coarse salt, sesame seeds, poppy seeds or leave plain. Cover loosely and allow to rise for 15 minutes in a warm place. Bake in a preheated hot oven (220°C, 425°F, gas 7) for about 15 minutes until golden brown and very crisp. Cool on a rack and store in an airtight container.

CHOLLAH

This is the traditional Jewish Sabbath loaf made without milk or butter.

250 ml/8 fl oz hand-hot water
450 g/1 lb strong plain flour
3 teaspoon caster sugar
15 g/½ oz fresh yeast or 1½ teaspoons dried yeast
2 teaspoons salt
2 tablespoons vegetable oil
1 egg, beaten
little egg yolk, to glaze
1 teaspoon poppy seeds

Place the water in a large bowl, add one-third of the flour (about 150 g/5 oz) all the sugar and the fresh or dried yeast. Mix until smooth, place inside a lightly oiled polythene bag and leave in a warm place until frothy (about 20 minutes). Now add the remaining flour, salt, oil and egg. Mix to a soft dough. Turn the dough out onto a lightly floured work surface and knead until smooth (about 10 minutes). Return to the lightly oiled polythene bag and leave in a warm place to rise until doubled in size about 1 hour (or for 12-24 hours in the refrigerator). Divide the dough into 4 pieces. Knead each into a ball; then roll each piece into a sausage about 30 cm/12 inches long. Press the strands firmly together at one end then plait tightly. Place on a lightly greased baking tray, return to the oiled polythene bag and leave to rise again until doubled in size, about 30 minutes. Brush with a little beaten egg and sprinkle with poppy seeds. Bake in a preheated hot oven (220°C, 425°F, gas 7) for 20-25 minutes.

BAGELS

These Jewish rolls are made from Chollah dough, but the rolls are boiled before being baked. Traditionally, they are split and filled with cream cheese and smoked salmon.

Follow the Chollah recipe, using an extra 50 g/2 oz flour. Knead and let rise once as for Chollah.

To shape the bagels, divide the dough into 20 pieces. Shape each piece into a ball and then roll into a sausage about 18 cm/7 inches long. Wind the rope around the knuckles of your hand and press on the table to seal it firmly. Allow to rise on a lightly greased baking tray placed inside a lightly oiled polythene bag until the bagels are puffy and larger in size (about 1 hour). They will not quite double in size.

Bring a large pan of water to the boil and drop 4 or 5 bagels at a time into the water. Boil for 2 minutes, turning them over with a spoon as they rise to the surface. Drain and lay on a board. Repeat with the remaining bagels. Place on a floured baking tray and bake in a preheated very hot oven (240°C, 475°F, gas 9) for 5 minutes. Turn them over and bake for a further 5 minutes until golden brown.

PITTA BREAD
Makes 12

Pitta bread comes from the Middle East and is very versatile. It can be torn into pieces and used as a dip or scoop with taramasalata or houmus; or when cut in half, it forms pockets which can be filled with kebabs, cold meats, salads, hard-boiled eggs or tuna.

**2 teaspoons dried yeast and 1 teaspoon sugar or
   15 g/½ oz fresh yeast
300 ml/½ pint hand-hot water
450 g/1 lb strong white flour
2 teaspoons salt
15 g/½ oz lard**

If using dried yeast, sprinkle the yeast and sugar onto the water and stir. Leave for 10-15 minutes until frothy. If using fresh yeast, blend the yeast with the water.

Sift the flour and salt into a large mixing bowl. Add the lard and rub in with the finger tips. Stir in the yeast liquid and mix to a dough. Turn the dough onto a lightly floured work surface and knead until the dough is firm and no longer sticky, about 10 minutes by hand or 5 minutes with an electric dough hook. Place the dough in a lightly oiled polythene bag and allow to rise in a warm place for about 1 hour or until doubled in size.

Knock back the risen dough and divide into 12 equal portions. Place 3 baking trays in a preheated hot oven (230°C, 450°F, gas 8). Roll each piece of dough into an oval 13-15 cm/5-6 inches long and lightly dust with flour. Place on the hot baking trays and bake for 8-10 minutes until the bread is well puffed up and just beginning to colour. Wrap in a cloth to keep the crust soft. Serve warm. To reheat pittas, warm in a hot oven, under the grill, in a toaster or on a barbecue for a few minutes before serving.

NAAN BREAD
Makes 6

In India these breads are cooked in very hot clay ovens called Tandoors, an alternative in this country is to use the grill.

**2 teaspoons dried yeast and 1 teaspoon sugar or
   15 g/½ oz fresh yeast
200 ml/7 fl oz hand-hot milk
450 g/1 lb plain white flour
½ teaspoon salt
1 teaspoon baking powder
2 teaspoons caster sugar
1 egg, beaten
2 tablespoons vegetable oil
4 tablespoons natural yogurt**

If using dried yeast, sprinkle the yeast and sugar onto the milk and stir. Leave for 10-15 minutes until frothy. If using fresh yeast, blend the yeast with the milk.

Mix the flour, salt, baking powder and sugar in a large mixing bowl. Add the egg, oil, yogurt and yeast liquid all at once to the flour and mix to a dough. Turn the dough onto a lightly floured work surface and knead until the dough is firm and no longer sticky, about 10 minutes by hand or 4 minutes with an electric dough hook. Place the dough in a lightly oiled polythene bag and allow to rise in a warm place until doubled in size, about 1 hour.

Knock back the dough and re-knead until firm. Divide the dough into six equal portions and roll each piece into an oval about 25 × 10 cm/10 × 4 inches. Place on greased baking trays. Preheat the grill until hot. Brush each naan with a little water and grill under a medium heat for 2-3 minutes until golden and puffy. Turn the naan over and grill until golden. Serve warm with Tandoori dishes.

Variations

SPICED NAAN
Work 1 teaspoon cumin seeds into the dough after the first rising.

STUFFED NAAN
Fry 1 tablespoon curry powder in 75 g/3 oz butter. Add 100 g/4 oz mashed potato and mix well. Spread the potato mixture over the rolled out naan. Fold over and roll out again. Grill as above.

PIZZA
Serves 1 to 2

This would be equally as good as the real pizza bought in Italy, if only we all had clay ovens. But this is as near as you can get. Add any one of the following toppings, or have bowls of ingredients ready for guests to make up their own for a pizza party.

15 g/½ oz fresh yeast or 1½ teaspoons dried yeast and 1 teaspoon sugar
100 ml/4 fl oz hand-hot water
200 g/7 oz strong plain flour
1 tablespoon olive oil
1 teaspoon salt

If using dried yeast, dissolve the sugar in the water. Sprinkle the yeast onto the water and stir. Leave for 10-15 minutes until frothy. If using fresh yeast, crumble the yeast into the water and stir until blended.

Sift the flour into a large bowl, make a well in the centre and add the yeast liquid, oil and salt. Mix together to form a soft dough. Turn the dough out onto a lightly floured work surface and knead until smooth, about 10 minutes. Place in a lightly oiled polythene bag and leave in a warm place until doubled in size, about 1 hour. Meanwhile prepare the topping.

Turn the dough onto a clean work surface and knock the dough back. Roll out to a circle about 25 cm/10 inches in diameter. With your fingers pinch a slightly thicker edge. Place on a lightly floured baking tray and add the desired topping. Bake in a preheated hot oven (220°C, 425°F, gas 7) for 20-25 minutes until bubbling and golden. Serve hot or cold.

Pizza toppings
BASIC TOMATO AND GARLIC

675 g/1½ lb tomatoes, peeled and chopped or
1 (396-g/14-oz) can plum tomatoes, drained and chopped
1 teaspoon sugar
5 tablespons olive oil
1 onion, peeled and chopped
1-2 cloves garlic, chopped (optional)
2 teaspoons dried oregano
salt and pepper

Place the tomatoes, sugar, 3 tablespoons of oil and the onion into a frying pan. Cook over a low heat for 15 minutes or until the sauce is thick and little excess moisture remains. Brush the pizza dough with a little of the remaining oil, top with the sauce, then garlic, oregano, and salt and pepper. Sprinkle with remaining oil. Bake as for main recipe.

TOMATO AND MOZZARELLA

1 quantity Basic Tomato and Garlic topping
5-6 fresh basil leaves or pinch of dried basil
1 mozzarella cheese about 200 g/7 oz
1 tablespoon grated Parmesan cheese
1 tablespoon olive oil
10 black olives

Pour the Basic Tomato and Garlic sauce over the pizza dough. Top with the basil. Thinly slice the mozzarella and arrange on top. Sprinkle with Parmesan and olive oil. Scatter with olives and bake as in the main recipe.

HAM AND MUSHROOM TOPPING

1 quantity Basic Tomato and Garlic topping
100 g/4 oz button mushrooms, sliced
100 g/4 oz ham, cut into strips
2 tablespoons olive oil
2 tablespoons grated Parmesan cheese
50 g/2 oz grated Cheddar cheese

Spread the Basic Tomato and Garlic topping over the pizza dough. Scatter with the mushrooms and ham. Sprinkle with oil, Parmesan and Cheddar cheeses. Bake as for main recipe.

CALZONE
Serves 1 to 2

An Italian version of our English pasty, calzone is bread dough oozing with salami and stringy mozzarella cheese!

1 quantity Pizza Dough
50 g/2 oz ricotta cheese or cottage cheese
75 g/3 oz Italian salami, finely diced
100 g/4 oz mozzarella cheese, chopped
pinch of dried oregano
3 tablespoons olive oil

Make and prove the dough as for the basic pizza recipe. Roll out to a 25-cm/10-inch circle as before. Mix the ricotta or cottage cheese with the salami, mozzarella, oregano, and 1 tablespoon olive oil. Brush the pizza dough with oil, place the filling onto one half of the dough leaving a 2.5-cm/1-inch border around the edge. Fold the dough over and seal the edges well. Place the calzone on a baking tray and brush with the remaining oil. Bake in a preheated hot oven (230°C, 450°F, gas 8) for 12-15 minutes until golden. Serve hot.

SCONE DOUGH PIZZA
Serves 2 to 4

Quick and easy to make for supper or lunch, this pizza is very filling too.

Base
225 g/8 oz wholewheat flour
pinch of salt
50 g/2 oz soft margarine
3 teaspoons baking powder
150 ml/¼ pint milk and water mixed
½ teaspoon sugar

Topping
4 tablespoons tomato purée
1 onion, peeled and grated
½ teaspoon dried mixed herbs
4 tomatoes, sliced
4 medium size mushrooms, sliced
50 g/2 oz Cheddar cheese, grated

Sift flour into a bowl and sprinkle the bran flakes from the sieve back into the bowl. Add the salt and the margarine and work it into the flour with a fork, until the mixture resembles fine breadcrumbs. Stir in the baking powder. Then add the milk and sugar and stir together to form a soft dough. Turn out on a lightly floured board and knead gently. Place on a floured baking tray and press out to a circle about 20 cm/8 inches in diameter.

   Spread the dough with tomato purée and top with grated onion and herbs. Arrange sliced tomatoes and mushrooms on top. Scatter with cheese. Bake in a preheated moderate oven (180°C, 350°F, gas 4) for 20 minutes. Serve hot or cold.

ONION BREAD
Makes 1 loaf

**1½ teaspoons dried yeast and 1 teaspoon sugar
   or 15 g/½ oz fresh yeast
200 ml/7 fl oz hand-hot milk
350 g/12 oz strong white flour
1 teaspoon salt
pinch of cayenne
25 g/1 oz lard or margarine
1 tablespoon oil
175 g/6 oz onions, sliced
egg glaze (see page 15)**

If using dried yeast, dissolve the sugar in the milk. Sprinkle the yeast onto the milk and stir. Leave for 10-15 minutes until frothy.

Sift the flour, salt and cayenne together into a bowl. If possible place in a warm oven for 5 minutes. Rub in the lard or margarine.

If using fresh yeast, crumble the yeast onto the hand-hot milk, and stir until blended. Pour the yeast liquid onto the flour and mix to a soft dough. Turn the dough out onto a lightly floured surface and knead until smooth and elastic, about 10 minutes by hand or 5 minutes with an electric dough hook. Place the dough in a lightly oiled polythene bag and loosely seal. Leave in a warm place to rise until doubled in size, about 1 hour.

Turn the dough onto a clean work surface and knock back until smooth. Shape the dough into a ball and place on a greased baking tray. Flatten the dough and slash across the top using a sharp knife. Cover loosely and leave in a warm place until again doubled in size or springy to the touch, about 30 minutes.

Fry the onions in the oil until soft but not brown. Drain. Brush the loaf with beaten egg and spoon the onions over the top. Bake in a preheated moderately hot oven (200°C, 400°F, gas 6) for 30-35 minutes or until the onions are golden and the loaf sounds hollow when tapped on the bottom. Cool on a rack.

GRECIAN OLIVE BREAD
Makes 1 large loaf

This delicious moist loaf has the rich flavour of olives. Use a virgin olive oil for the best flavour, although any good quality olive oil will do. Add green or black pitted olives or even a mixture of both.

**750 g/1½ lb strong white flour
2 teaspoons salt
1 sachet fast action or easy blend yeast
2 tablespoons sesame seeds
250 ml/½ pint hot water
150 ml/¼ pint olive oil
150 g/6 oz pitted olives, roughly chopped
1 teaspoon coarse sea salt**

Sift the flour and salt together into a large bowl. Stir in the yeast and sesame seeds. Mix the water and the oil together (it should then be hand-hot). Pour onto the flour and mix to a soft dough. Add the olives and mix well. Turn the dough out onto a lightly floured work surface and knead until smooth and elastic, about 10 minutes. Shape into a ball and place on a lightly greased baking tray. Press out to a 23-cm/9-inch circle. Place the baking tray inside a large oiled polythene bag. Leave in a warm place to rise until doubled in size and springy to the touch, about 1 hour. Brush the dough with a little water and sprinkle with the sea salt. Bake in a preheated hot oven (230°C, 450°F, gas 8) for 25-30 minutes until well risen and golden. Tap the base. If it sounds hollow, it is cooked. Cool on a wire rack.

CHEESE AND GARLIC BREAD

Makes 1 loaf or 8 rolls

If this bread is to be frozen, the garlic should be omitted. It can go rancid on storage and give an off flavour to the loaf.

**1½ teaspoons dried yeast and 1 teaspoon sugar
  or 15 g/½ oz fresh yeast
225 ml/8 fl oz hand-hot water
350 g/12 oz strong white flour
1 teaspoon salt
1 teaspoon mustard powder
25 g/1 oz lard or margarine
1 clove garlic, crushed
75 g/3 oz mature Cheddar, grated
50 g/2 oz grated Parmesan cheese**

topping
**25 g/1 oz mature Cheddar, grated
1 teaspoon cayenne**

If using dried yeast, dissolve the sugar in the milk. Sprinkle the yeast onto the water and stir. Leave for 10–15 minutes until frothy.

Sift the flour, salt and mustard powder together into a bowl. If possible place in a warm oven for 5 minutes. Rub in the lard or margarine.

If using fresh yeast, crumble the yeast onto the hand-hot water, stir until blended. Pour the yeast liquid onto the flour and mix to a soft dough. Turn the dough out onto a lightly floured surface and knead until smooth and elastic, about 10 minutes by hand or 5 minutes with an electric dough hook. Place the dough in a lightly oiled polythene bag and loosely seal. Leave in a warm place to rise until doubled in size, about 1 hour.

Turn the dough onto a clean work surface and knock back until smooth. Knead the garlic, Cheddar and Parmesan into the dough. To make a 'bumpy' loaf, divide the dough into five equal pieces. Shape each piece into a ball then squash it into an oblong to fit across the width of a 450-g/1-lb loaf tin. Fit all five pieces into the tin. To make rolls, see shapes pages 14–15. Cover loosely and leave in a warm place until again doubled in size, about 30 minutes.

Mix together the cheese and cayenne for the topping and sprinkle over the loaf or rolls. Bake in a preheated moderately hot oven (200°C, 400°F, gas 6) for 35–40 minutes for the loaf, until it sounds hollow when tapped on the bottom, and 20–25 minutes for the rolls. Cool on a rack.

ABERDEEN BUTTERIES
Makes 20

These are rich bread rolls rather like croissants. They are found in all bakers shops in the northeast of Scotland. Butter and lard are layered through the bread dough to give it a flaky texture. They are normally eaten warm for breakfast.

25 g/1 oz fresh yeast or 15 g/½ oz dried yeast
 and 1 teaspoon sugar
600 ml/1 pint hand-hot water
900 g/2 lb strong white flour
1 tablespoon salt
275 g/10 oz lard
275 g/10 oz butter

If using dried yeast, dissolve the sugar in 150 ml/¼ pint hand-hot water taken from the 600 ml/1 pint. Sprinkle the yeast onto the water and stir. Leave for 10–15 minutes until frothy. Then add the remaining water. Sift the flour and salt into a large bowl. If using fresh yeast crumble the yeast onto the hand-hot water and stir until blended. Pour the yeast liquid onto the flour; mix to a soft dough. Turn onto a lightly floured surface and knead until smooth and elastic about 10 minutes. Place the dough in a lightly oiled polythene bag and leave to rise until doubled in size, about 1 hour.

Mix the lard and butter together and chill. Turn the dough onto a clean work surface and knock back. Roll out to 36-cm × 15-cm/14-inch × 6-inch rectangle. Mark dough into thirds across the width. Spread a third of the fat on the top two-thirds of dough, then fold bottom third into the middle and fold top third over. Seal edges by pressing with a rolling pin. Cool for 10 minutes in the refrigerator.

Roll out pastry from short end and repeat process twice. After final rolling leave dough to rest for 10 minutes, then roll it out to 1-cm/½-inch thickness. Cut into squares and shape these into oval buns, turning in the edges. Place on a greased baking tray leaving space between each one and allow to rise for 30 minutes in a warm place until doubled in size. Bake in the top of a preheated moderately hot oven (200°C, 400°F, gas 6) for 15–20 minutes. Serve warm.

LIGHT RYE BREAD
Makes 1 large loaf

Rye bread, sliced thinly, makes an ideal base for open sandwiches.

1 tablespoon dried yeast and 1 teaspoon sugar
 or 25 g/1 oz fresh yeast
150 ml/6 fl oz hand-hot water
100 g/4 oz strong white flour
350 g/12 oz rye flour
1 teaspoon salt
15 g/½ oz lard
150 ml/¼ pint natural yogurt

If using dried yeast, dissolve the sugar in the water. Sprinkle the yeast onto the water and stir. Leave for 10–15 minutes until frothy.

Mix the flours and salt in a large mixing bowl. Rub in the lard. If using fresh yeast, crumble the yeast onto the hand-hot water; stir until blended. Pour the yeast liquid onto the flour with the yogurt and mix to form a dough. Turn onto a well floured surface and knead for 5 minutes. Place the dough in a lightly oiled polythene bag and loosely seal. Leave in a warm place until doubled in size, about 1¼ hours.

Knock back the dough and shape to fit a greased 1-kg/2-lb loaf tin (see Basic White Bread page 8). Cover loosely and allow to rise for about 35 minutes.

Bake in a preheated moderately hot oven (200°C, 400°F, gas 6) for 50 minutes. Remove the tin for the last 5 minutes of baking. Cool on a rack covered with a tea towel.

PUMPERNICKEL
Makes 1 large loaf or 2 small loaves

Don't worry if the loaf seems heavy and dense; it's meant to be. Keep for a day or two before slicing.

**2 teaspoons dried yeast and 1 teaspoon sugar or
    15 g/½ oz fresh yeast**
300 ml/½ pint hand-hot water
350 g/12 oz rye flour
250 g/9 oz plain brown flour
1 teaspoon salt
25 g/1 oz bran
100 g/4 oz potato, cooked and sieved
½ teaspoon caraway seeds
15 g/½ oz margarine
4 tablespoons molasses or black treacle

If using dried yeast, dissolve the sugar in the hand-hot water. Sprinkle the yeast onto the water and stir. Leave for 10–15 minutes until frothy.

Mix together the rye flour, brown flour, salt, bran, potato and caraway seeds. Rub in the margarine.

If using fresh yeast, crumble the yeast onto the hand-hot water and stir until blended. Pour the yeast liquid onto the flour with the molasses or black treacle and mix to form a stiff dough. Turn the dough onto a floured work surface and knead until the dough is firm, about 5 minutes. Place the dough in a lightly oiled polythene bag and loosely seal. Leave in a warm place until doubled in size, about 1½ hours.

Turn the risen dough onto a clean work surface and knock back until firm. Shape the dough to fit a 1-kg/2-lb greased loaf tin or two 450-g/1-lb greased loaf tins (see Basic White Bread page 8). Prick the surface of the dough all over with a skewer. Loosely cover and leave to rise again until doubled in size, about 45 minutes. Bake in a preheated moderate oven (180°C, 350°F, gas 4) for 1¼ hours for the large loaf and 50 minutes for the small loaves. Cool on a rack.

SWEET BREADS AND BUNS

CHELSEA BUNS
Makes 8 to 12 buns

**15 g/½ oz fresh yeast or 1½ teaspoons dried
   yeast and 1 teaspoon sugar
3½ tablespoons hand-hot milk
275 g/10 oz plain strong flour
pinch of salt
100 g/4 oz caster sugar
2 eggs, beaten
50 g/2 oz butter, melted but not hot
50 g/2 oz currants
50 g/2 oz glacé cherries, chopped
50 g/2 oz butter at room temperature
pinch of mixed spice**

If using dried yeast, dissolve 1 teaspoon sugar in the hand-hot milk. Sprinkle on the yeast. Stir. Leave for 10-15 minutes until frothy. If using fresh yeast, crumble the yeast onto the hand hot milk and stir well. Sift the flour and salt into a bowl. Mix in half the sugar, beaten eggs, yeast liquid and melted butter. Beat until smooth and elastic. Place the dough inside a lightly oiled polythene bag and leave in a warm place until doubled in size, about 45-50 minutes.

Turn the dough onto a clean work surface and knock it back. Allow the dough to rise again inside the polythene bag for a further 30 minutes. Turn the dough onto a floured work surface and roll it out to an oblong, about 30 cm by 13 cm/12 inches by 5 inches. Spread the remaining 50 g/2 oz butter over the top two-thirds of the dough. Fold the unbuttered third of the dough to the centre, and fold the other third down on top to make three layers. Press the edges with a rolling pin. Roll out again to about 45 cm/18 inches square. Sprinkle with the remaining sugar, currants, cherries and spice and roll up.

Cut the roll into eight to twelve slices and put them close together in a greased cake tin. Place inside a lightly oiled polythene bag and leave in a warm place until doubled in size, about 15-20 minutes. Bake in a preheated hot oven (220°C, 425°F, gas 7) for 20 minutes until golden. Sprinkle with caster sugar, if liked.

DOUGHNUTS
Makes 12

New oil should be used when frying doughnuts; otherwise they may take on unwanted flavours.

**225 g/8 oz strong white flour
2 teaspoons dried yeast or 15 g/½ oz fresh yeast
½ teaspoon sugar
75 ml/3 fl oz hand-hot milk
½ teaspoon salt
25 g/1 oz caster sugar
25 g/1 oz magarine
1 egg, beaten
caster sugar and ground cinnamon for tossing
   cooked doughnuts**

Sift 50 g/2 oz of the flour into a bowl. Stir the yeast and sugar into the milk. If using dried yeast, leave it to stand for 5 minutes. Mix with the flour and leave in a warm place until frothy, about 20 minutes.

Sift the remaining flour and salt into another mixing bowl. Stir in the sugar and rub in the margarine. Stir the flour mixture and the egg into the yeast batter and mix to a soft dough. Turn onto a well-floured work surface and knead until smooth and no longer sticky. Place in a lightly oiled polythene bag, loosely seal and leave in a warm place until doubled in size, about 1 hour.

Knock back the dough and roll out to 1 cm/½ inch thick. Cut into rings using a 7-cm/2¾-inch and a 4-cm/1½-inch plain cutter. Place on a greased tray,

cover loosely and allow the dough to rise again until springy to the touch, about 20 minutes.

Deep fry the doughnuts in hot oil 180°C/350°F until well browned, turning them frequently. Drain on absorbent kitchen paper and toss in caster sugar and cinnamon.

HOT CROSS BUNS
Makes 12

25 g/1 oz fresh yeast or 15 g/½ oz dried yeast
  and 1 teaspoon sugar
150 ml/¼ pint hand-hot milk
150 ml/¼ pint hand-hot water, less 4
  tablespoons
450 g/1 lb strong plain flour
1 teaspoon salt
½ teaspoon mixed spice
½ teaspoon ground cinnamon
½ teaspoon ground nutmeg
50 g/2 oz caster sugar
50 g/2 oz butter, melted but not hot
1 egg, beaten
100 g/4 oz currants
50 g/2 oz chopped mixed peel

Glaze
4 tablespoons milk and water mixed
40 g/1½ oz caster sugar

If using dried yeast, dissolve the sugar in 150 ml/ ¼ pint milk. Sprinkle on the yeast and leave for 10–15 minutes until frothy; then add the water. If using fresh yeast, crumble the yeast onto the milk and stir in the water.

Sift the flour and salt into a large bowl. If possible, place in a warm oven for 5 minutes. Add the spices and sugar. Stir the butter and egg into the yeast liquid and add it to the flour, with the fruit and peel. Mix to a soft dough. Turn onto a lightly floured work surface and knead until smooth and elastic, about 10 minutes. Place the dough in a lightly oiled polythene bag and loosely seal. Leave in a warm place to rise until doubled in size, for about 1 hour.

Turn the dough out onto a clean work surface and knock it back. Divide the dough into 12 equal pieces and shape into buns (see pages 14–15). Arrange them on a baking tray and place inside the oiled polythene bag to rise until doubled in size about 30 minutes. Using a razor sharp knife, cut a cross in the top of each bun and bake in a preheated moderately hot oven (190°C, 375°F, gas 5) for 15 to 20 minutes or until risen and brown.

To glaze, boil the milk, water and sugar together for 1 minute; then brush over the buns while they are still hot. Repeat if necessary; then allow to cool.

SAVARIN
Serves 6 to 8

**2 teaspoons dried yeast and 1 teaspoon sugar or
   15 g/½ oz fresh yeast
6 tablespoons hand-hot milk
175 g/6 oz strong white flour
½ teaspoon salt
2 eggs, size 3
75 g/3 oz butter**

syrup
**175 g/6 oz caster sugar
300 ml/½ pint water
thinly peeled rind of ½ lemon
juice of 1 lemon
3 tablespoons rum or brandy**

Grease a 900-ml/1½-pint ring mould and dust with flour. If using dried yeast, dissolve the sugar in the milk, sprinkle on the yeast and stir. Leave for 10-15 minutes until frothy.

Sift the flour and salt into a mixing bowl and make a well in the centre. If using fresh yeast, crumble the yeast onto the milk and stir until blended. Beat the eggs into the yeast liquid and pour into the centre of the flour. Sprinkle some of the flour from the sides over the liquid, cover and leave in a warm place for about 20 minutes until the yeast looks spongy.

Melt the butter and allow to cool until just warm. Add to the bowl and mix the ingredients together with a wooden spoon. Beat to make a soft batter. Pour into the prepared tin and spread level. Cover and leave for about 1 hour or until the mixture reaches the top of the tin. Bake in a preheated moderately hot oven (200°C, 400°F, gas 6) for 20-30 minutes until golden and firm. A skewer inserted

into the cake should come out clean. Cool for 5 minutes in the tin; then turn out and cool on a rack.

To make the syrup, gently heat the sugar with the water and lemon rind until the sugar has dissolved. Bring to the boil; then simmer for 5 minutes. Add the lemon juice and rum or brandy. Pour half the syrup into the cleaned ring mould and place the savarin back into the mould on the syrup. Carefully pour the remaining syrup over the top. Allow the syrup to soak in for about 15 minutes then chill until ready to serve. Turn onto a serving dish and serve with fresh fruit salad and whipped cream.

RUM BABAS
Makes 16 rum babas or 1 large savarin

This makes a light spongy dough which soaks up the rum syrup to make a sophisticated dessert.

**25 g/1 oz fresh yeast or 15 g/½ oz dried yeast
   and 1 teaspoon sugar
6 tablespoons warm milk
225 g/8 oz strong plain flour
½ teaspoon salt
2 tablespoons caster sugar
4 eggs, beaten
100 g/4 oz butter, softened
100 g/4 oz currants (optional)**

For the rum syrup
**8 tablespoons clear honey
8 tablespoons water
4 tablespoons dark rum
whipped cream to serve**

Lightly oil 16 9-cm/3½-inch ring moulds. Place the yeast, 1 teaspoon sugar if using dried yeast, milk and 50 g/2 oz of the flour into a bowl and blend until smooth. Allow to stand in a warm place until frothy, about 15-20 minutes. Add the remaining flour, salt, sugar, eggs, butter and currants. Beat well for 3-4

minutes. Half fill the moulds and place on a baking tray. Leave in a warm place until the dough has risen just to the top of the moulds. Bake in a preheated moderately hot oven (200°C, 400°F, gas 6) for 15-20 minutes. Cool for a few minutes then turn out and leave to cool on a wire rack. Heat the honey and water together in a small pan, remove from the heat and stir in the rum. Dip each baba into the hot syrup and leave to cool. Serve with whipped cream.

Note: If you have difficulty getting the babas out of their tins, soak them with the syrup first.

KUGELHOPF
Serves 16

This continental bread is generally eaten with coffee, but not tea. It is baked in a special fluted tin with a tube in the centre, known as a kugelhopf tin.

200 ml/7 fl oz hand-hot milk
25 g/1 oz fresh yeast or 15 g/½ oz dried yeast
   and 1 teaspoon sugar
350 g/12 oz flour
pinch of salt
25 g/1 oz caster sugar
2 eggs, size 3, beaten
100 g/4 oz butter, melted but not hot
50 g/2 oz currants
50 g/2 oz raisins or sultanas
24 blanched almonds
icing sugar (optional)

Butter a 1-litre/2-pint kugelhopf tin or ring mould. If using dried yeast, dissolve 1 teaspoon sugar in the milk, sprinkle on the yeast, stir. Leave for 5-10 minutes until frothy. Sift flour and salt into a bowl and place in a warm oven for 5 minutes. If using fresh yeast, crumble the yeast onto the hand-hot milk. Make a well in the centre of the flour, pour in the warm milk and yeast, add the sugar and eggs and the melted butter. Mix thoroughly together; then add the dried fruit. Press the blanched almonds round the sides and bottom of the buttered tin. Turn the dough into it so that it is three-quarters full; then place it inside a lightly oiled polythene bag and leave it in a warm place for about 20-30 minutes, or until the mixture is about 1 inch/2.5 cm below the top of the tin. Stand the tin on a thick baking sheet; then bake in the centre of a preheated moderately hot oven (200°C, 400°F, gas 6) for 50-60 minutes. If the top tends to colour too much, lower the heat until the kugelhopf is done. Leave for a few minutes before turning out. Dust with icing sugar if liked.

LEMON FIGGY RING
Serves 6 to 8

Dates can be used instead of figs if preferred.

175 g/6 oz strong white flour
2 teaspoons dried yeast or 15 g/½ oz fresh yeast
1 teaspoon sugar
5 tablespoons hand-hot milk
½ teaspoon salt
25 g/1 oz caster sugar
2 teaspoons grated lemon rind
25 g/1 oz butter
1 egg, beaten

filling
100 g/4 oz dried figs
1 tablespoon lemon juice

decoration
100 g/4 oz icing sugar
15 g/½ oz flaked almonds
4 glacé cherries, halved
2 slices fresh lemon, quartered

Sift 50 g/2 oz of the flour into a bowl. Stir the yeast and 1 teaspoon sugar into the milk. If using dried yeast let it stand for 5 minutes. Mix with the flour and leave in a warm place until frothy, about 20 minutes.

Sift the remaining flour and salt into another bowl. Stir in the sugar and lemon rind and rub in the butter. Stir the flour mixture and the egg into the yeast batter and mix to a soft dough. Turn onto a lightly floured surface and knead until smooth and no longer sticky. Place in a lightly oiled polythene bag, loosely seal and leave in a warm place until doubled in size, about 1 hour.

Knock back the dough and roll out to a rectangle 38 × 23 cm/15 × 9 inches. Place the dried figs and lemon juice in a food processor until finely chopped, or chop the figs by hand and stir in the lemon juice. Spread the fig mixture over the dough leaving a 1-cm/½-inch border all round. Roll up from the long side, like a Swiss roll and place on a greased baking tray. Join the ends together to form a ring and seal with a little water. Using scissors or a sharp knife cut almost through the dough at a 45° angle at 2.5-cm/1-inch intervals. Twist each section on its side to show the filling. Cover loosely and allow to rise again until springy to the touch, about 30 minutes.

Bake in a preheated moderately hot oven (200°C, 400°F, gas 6) for 25 minutes until golden. Cool on a rack.

To decorate, sift the icing sugar and mix with 2 tablespoons hot water to make a thick glacé icing. Spoon over the top of the cake and allow to dribble down the sides. Sprinkle with the almonds and decorate with the cherries and lemon. Cut into slices to serve.

MUESLI LOAF
Makes 1 loaf

Use unsweetened or sweetened muesli as preferred.

1 tablespoon dried yeast or 25 g/1 oz fresh yeast
1 teaspoon clear honey
200 ml/8 fl oz hand-hot milk
450 g/1 lb plain brown flour
1 teaspoon salt
50 g/2 oz butter or margarine
1 egg, beaten
175 g/6 oz muesli

Stir the yeast and honey into the milk. If using dried yeast allow to stand for 5 minutes. Mix in 100 g/4 oz flour and leave in a warm place until frothy, about 20 minutes.

Mix together the remaining flour and salt. Rub in the butter or margarine. Stir the flour mixture and the egg into the yeast batter and mix to a soft dough. Turn it onto a floured surface and knead until smooth and no longer sticky. Place in a lightly oiled polythene bag and loosely seal. Leave in a warm place to rise until doubled in size, about 1 hour.

Work the muesli into the risen dough until evenly distributed. Form into a loaf shape (see Basic White Bread page 8) and place in a greased 1-kg/2-lb loaf tin. Cover loosely and leave in a warm place until springy to the touch, about 1 hour.

Bake in a preheated moderately hot oven (200°C, 400°F, gas 6) for about 50 minutes, until golden and the loaf sounds hollow when tapped on the bottom. Cool on a rack. Serve sliced spread with butter and honey.

YORKSHIRE TEACAKES
Makes 5

These are good cut in half, toasted and served oozing with butter.

2 teaspoons dried yeast and 1 teaspoon sugar or
**   15 g/½ oz fresh yeast**
300 ml/½ pint hand-hot milk and water mixed
450 g/1 lb strong white flour
1 teaspoon salt
25 g/1 oz caster sugar
25 g/1 oz lard
50 g/2 oz currants
milk for brushing

If using dried yeast, dissolve the sugar in 150 ml/¼ pint hand-hot milk and water mixed taken from the 300 ml/½ pint. Sprinkle the yeast onto the milk and water and stir. Leave for 10–15 minutes until frothy.

Sift the flour and salt into a bowl. Add the sugar and rub in the lard. Add the yeast liquid with the remaining 150 ml/¼ pint milk and water.

If using fresh yeast, crumble the yeast onto the hand-hot water, stir until blended. Pour onto the flour and mix to a soft dough. Turn the dough onto a floured surface and knead until smooth and no longer sticky. Place the dough in a lightly oiled polythene bag and loosely seal. Leave in a warm place until doubled in size, about 1 hour.

Turn the dough onto a clean work surface and knock back until firm again. Work the currants into the dough. Divide into 5 equal pieces and shape each into a round cake 1 cm/½ inch thick. Place on greased baking trays and brush the tops with milk. Cover loosely and leave in a warm place until springy to the touch, about 50 minutes.

Bake in a preheated hot oven (220°C, 425°F, gas 7) for about 15 minutes until golden brown. Cool on a rack.

DEVON LARDY CAKE
Serves 12

This wickedly fattening cake is best eaten straight from the oven, warm, sticky and irresistible.

**15 g/½ oz fresh yeast or 1½ teaspoons dried
   yeast and 1 teaspoon sugar
300 ml/½ pint hand-hot water
450 g/1 lb strong plain flour
2 teaspoons salt
1 tablespoon oil
50 g/2 oz butter
100 g/4 oz caster sugar
1 teaspoon mixed spice
75 g/3 oz sultanas or currants
50 g/2 oz lard**

Lightly grease a roasting tin about 25 × 20 cm/10 × 8 inches. If using dried yeast, dissolve the sugar in 150 ml/¼ pint hand-hot water taken from the 300 ml/½ pint. Leave for 10-15 minutes until frothy; then add the remaining 150 ml/¼ pint water. If using fresh yeast, crumble the fresh yeast onto the water and stir until blended. Sift the flour and salt into a mixing bowl and stir in the yeast mixture with the oil to give a soft dough. Beat for 10 minutes or until smooth. Leave in a warm place to rise until doubled in size, about 1 hour.

Turn the dough out onto a lightly floured work surface and knock back. Knead for 5-10 minutes until smooth. Roll out into a rectangle about 5 mm/¼ inch thick. Dot the butter over two-thirds of the dough. Sprinkle half the sugar, spice and dried fruit over the dough. Fold the bottom third of the dough up towards the centre and fold the top third down. Seal the three edges firmly with a rolling pin then give the dough a one-half turn and roll out to an oblong again. Repeat the process with the lard and remaining sugar, spice and fruit. Fold and roll once more.

Place the dough in the tin punching it down to fill the tin. Place inside a large polythene bag and leave it to rise in a warm place for about 1 hour or until doubled in size. Brush with oil and sprinkle thickly with a little extra caster sugar. Score the top in a crisscross pattern. Bake in a preheated hot oven (220°C, 425°F, gas 7) for 30 minutes or until brown and sticky on top. Best served warm.

MUFFINS
Makes 12

A true old fashioned English tea wouldn't be the same without toasted muffins. If you have an open fire, toast them on a long-handled fork before eating. Otherwise toast them under a hot grill and spread with butter.

20 g/¾ oz fresh yeast or 2 teaspoons dried yeast and 1 teaspoon sugar
675 g/1½ lb strong plain flour
1 teaspoon salt
450 ml/¾ pint of hand-hot milk

If using dried yeast, dissolve 1 teaspoon sugar in 150 ml/¼ pint of hand-hot milk taken from the 450 ml/¾ pint. Sprinkle the yeast onto the milk and stir. Leave for 10-15 minutes until frothy. Add the remaining milk. Sift the flour and salt together.

If using fresh yeast, crumble the yeast onto the hand-hot milk and stir until blended.

Pour the yeast liquid onto the flour and mix to a soft dough. Place inside a lightly oiled polythene bag and allow to rise until doubled in size, about 1 hour.

Turn the dough onto a lightly floured work surface and knock back. Divide the dough into 12 pieces, form into small balls and flatten. Press them inside crumpet rings if you have them. Cook on a gently heated griddle or heavy based frying pan for about 5 minutes on each side or bake in a pre-heated moderately hot oven (190°C, 375°F, gas 5) for 20 minutes.

CRUMPETS
Makes 8

Light bubbly pancakes oozing with butter are the perfect tea time indulgence.

15 g/½ oz fresh yeast or 1½ teaspoons dried yeast and 1 teaspoon sugar
300 ml/½ pint hand-hot milk
225 g/8 oz strong plain flour
½ teaspoon salt
2 teaspoons brown sugar
oil for frying

If using dried yeast, dissolve 1 teaspoon sugar in 150 ml/¼ pint of hand-hot milk, taken from the 300 ml/½ pint. Sprinkle the yeast onto the milk and stir. Leave for 10-15 minutes until frothy. Add the remaining milk. Sift the flour and salt together. If using fresh yeast, crumble the yeast onto the milk. Stir until blended. Pour the yeast liquid onto the flour with the brown sugar and beat to a smooth batter. Place the bowl inside a lightly oiled polythene bag and leave in a warm place to rise until doubled in size, about 35-40 minutes.

Lightly grease a griddle or frying pan and 7.5-cm/3-inch crumpet rings or plain metal cutters. When the griddle or pan is hot, pour in the batter to half fill the rings. Cook over a moderate heat until set and the bubbles have burst. Remove the rings, turn, and cook for a further minute. Keep the crumpets in a warm oven while cooking the remaining batter. Serve with butter and a sprinkle of salt if liked.

SNOW BUNS
Makes 12 dumplings

These delicious snowy dumplings, often sold on the ski slopes in Austria, are filled with a figgy mixture. The secret is to steam them!

**25 g/1 oz fresh yeast or 15 g/½ oz dried yeast
  and 1 teaspoon sugar
150 ml/¼ pint hand-hot water
675 g/1½ lb strong plain flour
175 ml/6 fl oz hand-hot milk
1½ teaspoons vanilla essence
1 teaspoon grated lemon rind
100 g/4 oz sugar
1 teaspoon salt
3 egg yolks
1 egg white**

filling
**100 g/4 oz dried figs
6 canned apricot halves
3 tablespoons demerara sugar
1 teaspoon grated lemon rind**

lemon sauce
**100 g/4 oz unsalted butter
4 tablespoons lemon juice
2–3 tablespoons demerara sugar
2 teaspoons poppy seeds**

If using dried yeast, dissolve the sugar in the hand-hot water. Sprinkle the yeast onto the water and stir. Leave for 5 to 10 minutes until frothy. Sift the flour into a large bowl. If possible place in a warm oven for 5 minutes. If using fresh yeast, crumble the yeast onto the hand-hot water stir until blended. Mix the milk, vanilla essence, lemon rind, sugar and salt together; stir in egg yolks and whites. Add this and the yeast mixture to the flour. Stir until the mixture forms a soft dough. Turn onto a lightly floured work surface and knead until smooth, about 10 minutes. Place the dough inside a lightly oiled polythene bag and leave in a warm place to rise until doubled in size, about 45 minutes.

To make the filling, finely chop the figs and apricots, almost to a paste. Place in a bowl and add the sugar and lemon rind. Turn the dough onto a clean work surface and knock back. Knead for 2 to 3 minutes. Divide the dough into 12 pieces and roll or flatten each into a 10-cm/4-inch square. Place 1 tablespoon of filling in the centre of each and fold the dough over. Pinch the dough firmly to seal in the filling. Place the dumplings sealed side down on a greased baking tray. Cover with a cloth and leave in a warm place to rise for 10 minutes. Fill a large rectangular baking tin with water and place over the heat. Grease a wire cooling rack and place this over the roasting tin. Cover the rack with a sheet of greaseproof paper and place 6 dumplings on top. Cover the rack and buns with foil, making sure it doesn't touch the dumplings. Steam for 15-20 minutes until risen and cooked. Repeat with the remaining dumplings.

To make the sauce, melt the butter in a pan with the lemon juice and sugar. Pour over the dumplings and sprinkle with poppy seeds. Serve warm.

BARA BRITH
Serves 8

This famous "speckled bread" comes from Wales and is quite heavy but moist in texture and improves with keeping — if you can wait!

**25 g/1 oz fresh yeast or 15 g/½ oz dried yeast
    and 1 teaspoon sugar
300 ml/½ pint hand-hot milk
450 g/1 lb wholemeal flour
1 teaspoon salt
1 teaspoon mixed spice
75 g/3 oz butter
50 g/2 oz brown sugar
75 g/3 oz raisins
75 g/3 oz currants
25 g/1 oz candied peel
honey, to glaze**

Grease a 1-kg/2-lb loaf tin. If using dried yeast dissolve 1 teaspoon sugar in the milk and sprinkle on the yeast. Leave in a warm place until frothy, about 15 minutes. Meanwhile sift flour, salt and spice into a large bowl and rub in butter.

If using fresh yeast, crumble yeast onto the hand-hot milk. Make a well in the centre of the flour and add yeast mixture and brown sugar. Stir well. Turn onto a lightly floured work surface and knead until smooth and elastic. Place in a lightly oiled polythene bag and leave in warm place for about 1½ hours or until doubled in size.

Knock back and knead again, working in dried fruit and peel. Place in loaf tin and return to the polythene bag. Allow to rise again for 1½ hours or until doubled in size. Bake in a preheated moderately hot oven (200°C, 400°F, gas 6) for 45-60 minutes. Turn out and glaze with a little honey.

DEVONSHIRE SPLITS
Makes 12

Though you rarely see them these days, these scone-like bread rolls were once the traditional tea time fare filled with clotted cream and jam.

**15 g/½ oz fresh yeast or 1½ teaspoons dried
    yeast and 1 teaspoon sugar
300 ml/½ pint hand-hot milk
450 g/1 lb strong plain flour
40 g/1½ oz butter
15 g/½ oz caster sugar**

If using dried yeast, dissolve 1 teaspoon of sugar in 150 ml/¼ pint of the hand-hot milk taken from the 300 ml/½ pint. Sprinkle the yeast onto the milk and stir. Leave for 10 to 15 minutes until frothy. Then add the remaining milk. Sift the flour into a large mixing bowl and leave in a warm oven for 5 minutes if possible. If using fresh yeast, crumble the yeast onto the milk and stir until blended. Heat the butter gently until just melted, and not too hot. Add the yeast liquid, butter, and sugar to the flour and mix to a smooth dough. Turn onto a lightly floured work surface and knead until smooth, about 10 minutes. Place dough inside a lightly oiled polythene bag and leave in a warm place to rise until doubled in size, about 1 hour.

Turn the dough onto a clean work surface and knock back. Divide the dough into 12 pieces, and shape each into a ball. Place on a lightly greased baking tray and leave to prove in the polythene bag until doubled in size again, about 30 minutes. Bake in a preheated hot oven (220°C, 425°F, gas 7) for 15 to 20 minutes until golden. Allow to cool. Split and fill with cream and jam.

DANISH PASTRIES
Makes 12

Traditionally made in various shapes, Danish pastries can be filled with almond paste, jam, sultanas and raisins, or vanilla custard, or whatever variations you desire.

**25 g/1 oz fresh yeast or 15 g/½ oz dried yeast
  and 1 teaspoon sugar
150 ml/¼ pint hand-hot milk
250 g/9 oz butter
1 egg, beaten
50 g/2 oz caster sugar
350 g/12 oz strong plain flour
pinch of salt
beaten egg, for glazing**

glaće icing
**8 tablespoons icing sugar
2–3 tablespoons warm water**

If using dried yeast, dissolve 1 teaspoon sugar in the hand-hot milk and sprinkle the yeast onto the milk. Stir. Leave for 10–15 minutes until frothy. If using fresh yeast, crumble the yeast onto the hand-hot milk. Stir. Gently melt 50 g/2 oz of the butter and stir in the yeast mixture with the beaten egg and caster sugar. Sift the flour and into a large bowl. Add the yeast liquid and mix to a soft dough. Place inside a lightly oiled polythene bag and leave in a warm place to rise until doubled in size, about 1 hour.

Turn the dough onto a lightly floured work surface and knock back. Knead the dough lightly, then roll it out to an oblong about 35 × 15 cm/14 × 6 inches. Dot half the remaining butter in small pieces over two-thirds of the dough. Fold the unbuttered third of the dough into the centre, then fold the other third over that. Seal the three edges with a rolling pin and press down lightly in the centre. Give the dough a half turn and roll it out to its original oblong size. Place on a plate and chill for 10–15 minutes.

Fold in three and roll out again. Dot with remaining butter. Fold and chill for 15 minutes. Repeat the rolling and chilling at least twice more. Roll out the dough until it is 1 cm/½ inch thick; then shape and fill as described below. Prove and bake in a preheated moderately hot oven (200°C, 400°F, gas 6) for 25 minutes.

To make the icing, mix the sugar with enough water to just give a pouring consistency. Dribble the glaće icing over the pastries if liked.

CARTWHEELS

Roll out the Danish pastry dough as thinly as possible to a large oblong, spread carefully with a thin layer of Almond Filling, then sprinkle with raisins and roll it up as for a Swiss roll. Cut the roll into 6-mm/¼-inch slices, and place the slices, cut side down, on a greased baking tin. Prove, brush with beaten egg, and sprinkle flaked almonds on the top before baking.

PINWHEELS

Roll out dough thinly and cut it into 10-cm/4-inch squares. Cut the dough from each corner to within 1 cm/½ inch of the centre. Fold four alternate points to the centre, pressing them down firmly. Put a little jam or Almond Filling in the centre, then prove and bake.

CRESCENTS

Roll dough into a large circle 3 mm/⅛ inch thick, and cut it into triangles or wedges. Pour a little Almond Filling on each triangle and roll it up loosely, starting at the base of the triangle, and then shape into crescents. Prove and bake.

ENVELOPES

Roll out the dough thinly and cut into 10-cm/4-inch squares. Spread with Vanilla Cream and fold the corners in towards the middle. Press the edges down lightly. Prove, then bake for 12-15 minutes. Brush lightly with glacé icing.

COMBS

Roll out the dough fairly thinly, and cut into strips about 13 cm/5 inches wide. Place Apple Filling or Almond Filling in the middle, and fold both sides over. Brush lightly with beaten egg and roll in crushed lump sugar and chopped almonds. Cut into pieces about 4 inches long and gash four or five times on one side; open out the slits slightly. Prove, then bake for 12-15 minutes. These combs can be brushed slightly with beaten egg before baking to give them a glazed finish.

VANILLA CREAM

1 tablespoon flour
1 teaspoon cornflour
1 egg yolk
1 tablespoon sugar
150 ml/¼ pint milk
2-3 drops of vanilla essence

Work the flours, egg yolk and sugar together, adding a little milk. Bring the rest of the milk to the boil, pour onto the mixture, blend and return to the pan. Stir until boiling. Allow to cool, then flavour with a few drops of vanilla essence.

ALMOND FILLING

50 g/2 oz almonds, ground
50 g/2 oz caster sugar
little beaten egg

Mix the almonds and sugar together and bind with enough egg to bring to a firm paste.

APPLE FILLING

This can be used for any shape of Danish pastries and the pastries can either be finished with a soft icing or brushed with a little apricot glaze.

225 g/8 oz cooking apples
15 g/½ oz butter
grated rind and juice of ½ lemon
2 tablespoons granulated sugar

Wipe the apples, quarter and core them, but do not peel. Rub the butter round a saucepan, slice in the apples and add the grated rind and lemon juice. Cover and cook them slowly to a pulp. Rub pulp through a nylon strainer, return to the rinsed out pan with the sugar. Cook gently until thick. Turn out and allow to get quite cool before using.

STOLLEN
Makes 1 loaf

The way in which the dough is folded in this traditional German Christmas cake represents Jesus wrapped in swaddling clothes.

yeast batter
15 g/½ oz fresh yeast or 2 teaspoons dried yeast
½ teaspoon sugar
4½ tablespoons hand-hot milk
50 g/2 oz strong white flour

other ingredients
175 g/6 oz strong white flour
½ teaspoon salt
25 g/1 oz caster sugar
40 g/1½ oz butter
1 egg, beaten
25 g/1 oz chopped nuts
grated rind of 1 lemon
50 g/2 oz currants
50 g/2 oz sultanas
15 g/½ oz mixed peel
50 g/2 oz glacé cherries
icing sugar, for dredging

To make the batter, stir the yeast and sugar into the milk. If using dried yeast allow it to stand for 5 minutes. Mix in the flour and leave in a warm place until frothy, about 20 minutes.

To make the dough, mix together the flour, salt and sugar. Rub in 25 g/1 oz of the butter. Stir the flour mixture and the egg into the yeast batter and mix to a soft dough. Turn onto a floured work surface and knead until smooth and no longer sticky, about 10 minutes or 5 minutes with an electric dough hook. Place in a lightly oiled polythene bag, loosely seal and leave in a warm place until doubled in size, about 1 hour.

Squeeze the nuts, lemon rind and fruit, except the cherries, into the risen dough. On a floured surface roll out the dough to a circle 25 cm/10 inches in diameter. Melt the remaining butter and brush half of it over the dough. Spread the cherries down the centre and fold the dough into three to cover the cherries. Press lightly together and place on a greased baking tray. Brush with melted butter, cover loosely and allow to rise for about 30 minutes. Bake in a preheated moderately hot oven (200°C, 400°F, gas 6) for about 35-40 minutes. Cool on a rack. Dredge with icing sugar. Serve sliced.

PISTACHIO BREAD
Makes 1 small loaf

This sweet bread can be served as an accompaniment to ice cream or fresh fruit.

4 teaspoons dried yeast and 1 teaspoon sugar or 25 g/1 oz fresh yeast
6 tablespoons hand-hot milk
225 g/8 oz strong white flour
1 teaspoon salt
50 g/2 oz caster sugar
50 g/2 oz butter
75 g/3 oz shelled pistachio nuts, roughly chopped
icing sugar, for dredging

Sift 50 g/2 oz of the flour into a bowl. Stir the yeast and 1 teaspoon of sugar into the milk. If using dried yeast, leave it to stand for 5 minutes. Mix with the flour and leave in a warm place until frothy, about 20 minutes.

Sift the remaining flour and salt into another bowl. Stir in the sugar and rub in the butter. Stir the flour mixture into the yeast batter and mix to a soft dough. Turn onto a floured surface and knead until smooth and elastic. Place the dough in a lightly oiled polythene bag and loosely seal. Leave in a warm place until doubled in size, about 1½ hours.

Knock back the dough and work in the pistachio nuts. Shape the dough to fit a greased 450-g/1-lb loaf

tin (see Basic White Bread page 8). Cover loosely and allow to rise until springy to the touch about 45 minutes.

Bake in a preheated moderately hot oven (200°C, 400°F, gas 6) for about 35 minutes until golden. Cool on a rack. Dredge with icing sugar. Serve thinly sliced and buttered.

POPPY SEED ROLL
Serves 12

This delicious moist dough has a tangy poppy seed filling that once tasted, we know you'll love. Do try to grind the poppyseeds if you can, if not, use less milk, to give a soft poppy paste.

15 g/½ oz fresh yeast or 1½ teaspoons dried yeast and 1 teaspoon sugar
200 ml/7 fl oz milk
450 g/1 lb strong plain flour
pinch of salt
75 g/3 oz butter or margarine, melted but not hot
1 egg, beaten
75 g/3 oz caster sugar
2 drops of vanilla essence

filling
100 g/4 oz poppy seeds
100 g/4 oz walnuts, finely chopped
rind and juice of 1 lemon
1 egg
75 g/3 oz sugar
2 tablespoons flour
drop of vanilla essence

If using dried yeast, dissolve 1 teaspoon sugar in the hand-hot milk. Sprinkle on the yeast. Leave for 10-15 minutes until frothy. If using fresh yeast, crumble the yeast onto the milk and stir well.

Sift the flour and salt into a bowl, make a well in the centre and pour in the yeast liquid, melted butter or margarine, egg, sugar and vanilla essence. Beat until smooth, turn onto a lightly floured work surface and knead until smooth, about 10 minutes. Place the dough inside a lightly oiled polythene bag and leave in a warm place to rise until doubled in size about 30 minutes.

Mix the filling ingredients together. Turn the dough out onto a clean work surface and knock it back. Roll the dough on a clean kitchen towel dusted with flour to an oblong about 45 × 30 cm/18 × 12 inches. Spread the filling over and roll up the dough like a Swiss roll, using the tea towel to support the dough. Place the dough in a 20-cm/8-inch round springform ring mould. Press the dough to the edges, then snip the top with scissors. Leave in a warm place to rise for 30 minutes. Bake in a preheated moderately hot oven (200°C, 400°F, gas 6) for 10 minutes; then reduce oven temperature to (190°C, 375°F, gas 5) for 30-40 minutes. Cover with greaseproof paper if the top begins to get too brown. Allow to cool. Sprinkle with icing sugar if liked. Serve sliced.

NON-YEAST BREADS AND SCONES

SODA BREAD
Makes 1 loaf

A quick and easy to make loaf that is best eaten the day it is made.

675 g/1½ lb plain flour *or* 350 g/12 oz plain flour
**   and 350 g/12 oz wholemeal flour**
1½ teaspoons salt
1½ teaspoons bicarbonate of soda
2 teaspoons cream of tartar
40 g/1½ oz butter
450 ml/¾ pint milk

Sift the flour, salt, bicarbonate of soda and cream of tartar together in a large bowl. Rub in the butter and stir in the milk to give a soft dough. Turn out the dough onto a lightly floured work surface and shape into a large round about 5 cm/2 inches thick. Place on a baking tray and score the top into quarters. Bake in a preheated moderately hot oven (200°C, 400°F, gas 6) for 25-30 minutes until risen and golden brown. Tap the base of the soda bread; if it sounds hollow it is cooked.

SCOTTISH OATCAKES
Makes 16 biscuits

These thin crisp biscuits are best when eaten with cheese. Roll out the mixture while it is still warm, or you will find it difficult to handle.

100 g/4 oz fine oatmeal
7 g/¼ oz lard
pinch of salt
pinch of bicarbonate of soda

Place a griddle or flat heavy based frying pan on a low heat to warm. Melt the lard in 3 to 4 tablespoons boiling water. Place the oatmeal in a bowl with the salt and bicarbonate of soda. Mix in the lard and water to give a firm dough. Turn out onto a work surface dusted with oatmeal and quickly roll it into two circles about 3 mm/⅛ inch thick. Cut each circle into eight triangles and bake on the griddle or frying pan until they begin to dry out and the corners begin to curl up. Store in a biscuit tin. Heat in a warm oven for a few minutes before serving.

DROP SCONES
Makes about 30

A wonderfully quick treat, these should be cooked on a griddle or heavy based frying pan and eaten while still warm with butter, honey or syrup.

150 g/5 oz plain flour
1 large pinch of salt
2 teaspoons baking powder
2–3 teaspoons caster sugar
1 egg
25 g/1 oz butter, melted
150 ml/¼ pint milk

Heat the griddle or heavy based frying pan over a moderate heat. Sift the flour, salt and baking powder into a large bowl. Add the sugar. Make a well in the centre and drop in the egg and melted butter. Gradually add the milk, mixing with a wooden spoon to give a thick smooth batter. Pour the mixture into a measuring jug.

Lightly grease the griddle or pan and pour on little pools of the mixture to give perfectly round cakes. As soon as the cakes are puffed and full of bubbles and the underside brown, flip them over with a palette knife to brown the other side. Serve warm.

GRIDDLE SCONES
Makes 8

A griddle or girdle is a flat heavy cast iron plate used to cook scones and flat breads. A heavy based frying pan will do just as well. The secret of cooking on a griddle or pan is to preheat it to the right temperature first. Don't let it get too hot or the outside of the scones will be cooked before the centre. A good test is to sprinkle the griddle with flour, if it turns brown in 3 minutes the griddle is at the correct temperature.

225 g/8 oz plain or wholewheat flour
large pinch of salt
1 level teaspoon of bicarbonate of soda
1 teaspoon caster sugar
50 g/2 oz butter or margarine
1 tablespoon currants (optional)
2 teaspoons cream of tartar
150 ml/¼ pint milk

Heat the griddle. Sift the flour, salt, and bicarbonate of soda into a large bowl. Stir in the sugar and rub in the butter or margarine. Add the currants if using. Stir the cream of tartar into the milk and pour onto the flour. Mix it quickly together to give a firm but soft dough. Turn the dough out onto a lightly floured work surface and cut in half. Shape each piece into a round about 1 cm/½ inch thick and cut into quarters. Dust with flour and cook on the hot griddle or pan for about 5 minutes on each side or until risen and golden brown. Serve warm, split and buttered.

WHOLEWHEAT SCONES
Makes 8 scones

This is the quickest and lightest wholewheat scone recipe I have ever made — perfect every time.

225 g/8 oz wholewheat flour
pinch of salt
50 g/2 oz soft margarine
142 ml/5 fl oz natural yogurt
1 teaspoon bicarbonate of soda

Mix the flour and salt together, add the margarine and work it into the flour with a fork, until the mixture resembles breadcrumbs. Pour the yogurt into a bowl, stir in the bicarbonate of soda and leave for 2 minutes until frothy. Stir the yogurt into the flour, and knead lightly to a soft dough. Roll out on a floured work surface to a thickness of 1 cm/½ inch and cut out scones using a 5-cm/2-inch fluted pastry cutter. Place on a greased baking tray and bake in a preheated hot oven (220°C, 425°F, gas 7) for 10 minutes until risen. Cool on a wire rack.

Variations

CHEESE SCONES

Add 50 g/2 oz mature Cheddar, grated and 2 teaspoons whole grain mustard to the Wholewheat Scones recipe.

BACON AND SUNFLOWER SCONES

Add 4 tablespoons sunflower seeds to the basic dough with 4 rashers chopped fried bacon.

RAISIN AND PEANUT SCONES

Add 25 g/1 oz raisins and 25 g/1 oz peanuts and 1 tablespoon honey to the Wholewheat Scones recipe.

OVEN SCONES
Makes 10 to 12

These traditional English scones are best served on the day of making with clotted cream and strawberry jam.

50 g/2 oz butter or margarine
225 g/8 oz self raising flour★
½ teaspoon salt
150 ml/¼ pint milk

Rub the fat into the flour and salt until the mixture resembles fine breadcrumbs. Stir in enough milk to give a soft dough. Turn onto a lightly floured board and knead gently. Pat out to about 2.5 cm/1-inch thick and stamp out circles using a 5-cm/2-inch fluted round pastry cutter. Place on a floured baking tray and brush with a little beaten egg or milk if liked. Bake in a preheated hot oven (230°C, 450°F, gas 8) for 8-10 minutes until golden.

★If using plain flour, add 3 teaspoons of baking powder to 225 g/8 oz flour or 2 teaspoons cream of tartar plus 1 teaspoon bicarbonate of soda.

Variations

FRUIT SCONES

Add 50 g/2 oz sultanas, raisins, currants, or chopped dates to the dry ingredients with 2-3 tablespoons caster sugar.

RICH TEA SCONES

Add 2-3 tablespoons caster sugar to the dried ingredients and use 1 beaten egg with 1-2 tablespoons milk instead of all milk. Mix as for basic oven scones.

APPLE AND CINNAMON SCONES

Add 1 peeled and grated apple, ½ teaspoon cinnamon and 1 tablespoon runny honey to the dry ingredients. Mix as basic oven scones.

CURRIED SCONES

Add a pinch of sugar, 2 tablespoons fruit chutney and 1 tablespoon mild curry powder to the dry ingredients. Mix as for basic oven scones. These scones are delicious with cheese for a light lunch.

CHAPATI
Makes about 15

These are the basic flat Indian breads made from wholewheat flour and eaten with most Indian meals. They are traditionally cooked on a tava, a circular concave plate, but a heavy frying pan is fine. They are quick to cook and are delicious served with butter as a snack.

250 g/9 oz wholewheat flour
175 ml/6 fl oz water

Sift the flour into a large bowl and discard the bran flakes. Gradually stir in the water. The mixture should form a soft dough, so do not be afraid to add more water if necessary. Turn the dough onto a clean work surface and knead for 6 to 8 minutes until smooth. Place the dough in a bowl and cover with a clean damp tea towel for 30 minutes.

Place a heavy based frying pan over a moderate heat for 10 minutes until it is very hot, then turn the heat to low. Knead the dough again and cut it into 15 equal pieces. Roll each piece between lightly floured hands into a ball, then roll on a well-floured work surface into a circle about 14 cm/5 inches in diameter. Pat it between your hands to shake off the excess flour; then place it in the frying pan. Cook for 1 minute until the underside develops white spots. Turn the chapati over and cook the other side for half a minute. Remove the pan from the heat and, using metal tongs, flip the chapati onto the actual gas flame or electric ring just for a second. This will make it puff up, but is not essential. Stack the chapatis between a clean tea towel until all are cooked. Serve hot.

To make in advance, store chapati wrapped in foil for 1 day or freeze for up to 3 months. Reheat wrapped in foil in a hot oven (220°C, 425°F, gas 7) for 15-20 minutes or 30 minutes if frozen.

POTATO SCONES
Makes about 12

These are moist with a potato sweetness which is delicious eaten cold, or fried for breakfast. You can add a little sugar to make them sweeter if you prefer, or even nicer, just add a few plump sultanas for tea time. A little grated mature Cheddar cheese is also good for savoury cocktail nibbles.

675 g/1½ lb floury, boiled cold potatoes
pinch of salt
175 g/6 oz plain flour

Mash or sieve the potatoes well. Place in a large bowl and add salt to taste. Gradually work in the flour, kneading the dough lightly and carefully. Roll out the mixture on a lightly floured work surface, to a thickness of about 5 mm/¼ inch. Cut into rounds the size of a dinner plate and then cut into quarters, or using a plain pastry cutter, cut into 5-cm/2-inch circles. Bake on a lightly greased moderately hot griddle or heavy based frying pan for 4-5 minutes on each side. Serve warm.

PARATHA
Makes 12

Parathas can be frozen and re-heated as required. Simply stack interleaved with baking parchment, place in a freezer bag and seal. To re-heat, separate the parathas and warm in a moderately hot oven (200°C, 400°F, gas 6) for 10-15 minutes.

350 g/12 oz wholemeal flour
350 g/12 oz plain flour
2 teaspoons salt
100 g/4 oz butter
450 ml/¾ pint warm water

Mix the flours and salt together in a bowl; rub in 25 g/1oz of the butter. Add the warm water and mix to make a firm dough. Turn out onto a lightly floured surface and knead for 5 minutes. Wrap in a polythene bag and leave to rest for 1 hour.

Divide the dough into 12 equal portions. Roll one piece into a ball in the hands. Roll out on a lightly floured surface to an 18-cm/7-inch round. Make a cut from the centre to the outer edge and starting at a cut edge roll the dough tightly into a cone shape. Squash the cone slightly to form a rough round then roll out again to a flat round. Repeat with the remaining pieces of dough. Melt the remaining butter. Brush a thin layer of melted butter over a heavy frying pan. Fry the parathas one at a time for about 2 minutes, brushing them with more butter and turning once. Serve warm with curries, spiced kebabs or Tandoori dishes.

TEA CAKES

Who can resist a slice of cake? We know we're all supposed to be watching our weight, but when it's home-made and full of goodness, what's the harm? When you need something filling and sweet, a home-made cake is better than a chocolate bar and more satisfying. Dried fruit is naturally sweet, and nuts give you protein too. A slice of cake is great in a packed lunch, when the kids come home from school, or when you need a pick-me-up at any time of the day.

MADEIRA CAKE
Makes one 15-cm/6-inch square cake

This cake makes an excellent base for novelty cakes. It is firm to cut and will keep for about 3 weeks.

100 g/4 oz butter
100 g/4 oz caster sugar
2 eggs, size 3
100 g/4 oz self raising flour
50 g/2 oz plain flour
1 teaspoon finely grated lemon rind
2 teaspoons lemon juice

Grease a 15-cm/6-inch square cake tin and line the base with greased greaseproof paper. Cream the butter and sugar together until light and fluffy. Gradually beat in the eggs, adding a spoonful of flour if the mixture starts to curdle. Sift the flours together and fold into the creamed mixture with the lemon rind and juice. Spoon into the prepared tin and level the top with the back of a spoon. Bake in a preheated moderate oven (160°C, 325°F, gas 3) for about 1 hour until golden, firm to the touch and beginning to shrink from the sides of the tin. Allow to cool in the tin for 15 minutes; remove the tin and paper and cool on a rack.

GOLDEN MALT LOAF
Serves 8

Fruity and sticky, this loaf is best served spread with butter and eaten with a little cheese.

225 g/8 oz plain flour
1 teaspoon baking powder
1 teaspoon salt
175 g/6 oz raisins or sultanas
300 ml/½ pint milk
2 teaspoons honey
3 tablespoons malt extract

Grease and line a 450-g/1-lb loaf tin with greased greaseproof paper. Sift the flour and baking powder

into a large bowl. Add the salt and fruit. Warm the milk, honey and malt together in a pan over a low heat until just hand-hot. Pour onto the flour and beat well to give a soft dough. Pour into the prepared tin and bake in a preheated moderate oven (160°C, 325°F, gas 3) for about 1 hour. The mixture will dip slightly in the centre. Allow to cool. Store in a tin for up to 1 week.

CHERRY ALMOND CAKE
Makes one 20-cm/8-inch round cake

To stop the cherries sinking to the bottom, rinse them well to remove the syrup and then dry on absorbent kitchen paper.

100 g/4 oz glacé cherries
100 g/4 oz butter or margarine, softened
225 g/8 oz caster sugar
3 eggs, size 3
¼ teaspoon almond essence
225 g/8 oz self raising flour
100 g/4 oz ground almonds
25 g/1 oz flaked almonds
2 teaspoons granulated sugar

Grease a 20-cm/8-inch loose-bottomed round cake tin and line the base and sides with greased greaseproof paper. Rinse the cherries to remove the syrup, cut in half and dry on absorbent kitchen paper. Cream together the butter or margarine and caster sugar until light and fluffy. Beat the eggs with the almond essence and gradually add to the creamed mixture, beating well after each addition. Add the cherries and mix thoroughly. Fold in the flour and ground almonds, using a metal spoon. Spoon the mixture into the prepared tin and smooth the top with the back of a spoon. Sprinkle the flaked almonds over the cake mixture, then sprinkle the granulated sugar on top. Bake in a preheated cool oven (150°C, 300°F, gas 2) for about 2 hours until well risen, golden and firm to the touch. Cool in the tin for 30 minutes; then turn out and remove the paper. Cool on a rack.

PINEAPPLE RAISIN TEA BREAD
Makes one 1-kg/2-lb loaf

This moist cake is easy to make.

175 g/6 oz self raising wholemeal flour
175 g/6 oz self raising white flour
pinch of salt
1 teaspoon cinnamon
50 g/2 oz soft light brown sugar
50 g/2 oz butter or margarine
2 eggs, size 3, beaten
150 ml/¼ pint milk
1 (227-g/8-oz) can pineapple rings, drained
50 g/2 oz raisins

Mix the flours, salt, cinnamon and sugar together. Rub in the butter or margarine. Gradually beat in the eggs and milk. Chop the pineapple and stir into the mixture with the raisins. Spoon mixture into a greased 1-kg/2-lb loaf tin and bake in a preheated moderate oven (160°C, 325°F, gas 3) for 1 hour until golden brown and firm to the touch. A skewer inserted into the centre should come out clean. Leave in the tin for 10 minutes then cool on a rack.

COCONUT ROCKIES
Makes 18

Brown flour and sugar can be used instead of white.

225 g/8 oz plain flour
pinch of salt
1½ teaspoons baking powder
75 g/3 oz butter or margarine
50 g/2 oz caster sugar
50 g/2 oz desiccated coconut
1 egg, beaten
75 ml/3 fl oz milk

Sift the flour, salt and baking powder in a bowl. Rub in the butter until the mixture resembles fine breadcrumbs. Stir in the sugar and coconut. Add the beaten egg and mix with a fork; add sufficient milk to make a stiff mixture. Place small heaps of mixture on greased baking trays. Bake in a preheated hot oven (220°C, 425°F, gas 7) for 10–15 minutes until golden brown. Cool on a rack.

DUNDEE CAKE
Makes 1 20-cm/8-inch cake
Serves 12 to 15

Make this cake a few days or even a week in advance;
it will cut better and taste deliciously moist.

275 g/10 oz plain flour
1½ teaspoons baking powder
½ teaspoon salt
50 g/2 oz ground almonds
175 g/6 oz butter
50 g/2 oz white cooking fat
225 g/8 oz soft brown sugar
4 eggs, beaten
finely grated rind of 1 lemon
350 g/12 oz sultanas
225 g/8 oz currants
100 g/4 oz chopped, mixed peel
about 18 blanched almond halves

Sift the flour, baking powder and salt together; mix
in the ground almonds and set aside. In a mixing
bowl, cream the butter, white cooking fat and sugar
until soft and fluffy. Gradually beat the eggs into the
creamed mixture a little at a time. Add a little of the
flour with the last few additions of egg. Then, using a
metal spoon, fold in first the remaining flour then the
lemon rind, dried fruit and peel. Spoon the mixture
into a greased and lined 20-cm/8-inch round deep
cake tin. Spread the mixture level and hollow out the
centre slightly. Bake in a preheated moderate oven at
(180°C, 350°F, gas 4) and bake for 30 minutes. Then,
without removing the cake from the oven, carefully
place the almond halves over the top of the cake and
bake for a further 15 minutes. Lower the oven heat to
(160°C, 325°F, gas 3) and bake for a further 1¾ hours
(2½ hours of cooking time in all). Cool the cake in
the tin before turning out.

APRICOT CRYSTAL CAKE
Serves 12

Everything good that we could think of all in one cake!

225 g/8 oz butter or margarine
100 g/4 oz soft brown sugar
4 eggs, beaten
175 g/6 oz wholewheat flour
pinch of salt
100 g/4 oz ground almonds
175 g/6 oz glaće cherries
150 g/5 oz no-need-to-soak apricots, chopped
150 g/5 oz dried figs, chopped
225 g/8 oz mixed nuts
100 g/4 oz stem ginger, drained and chopped
2 tablespoons golden syrup
grated rind and juice of 1 orange
2-3 tablespoons milk

Grease and line a 20-cm/8-inch square cake tin with greased greaseproof paper. Cream the butter and sugar until light and fluffy. Gradually beat in the egg, adding a little flour if the mixture begins to curdle. Stir in the flour and salt, mix well then add the remaining ingredients. Stir well and place into prepared cake tin. Smooth the top with the back of a spoon and bake in the centre of a preheated moderate oven (180°C, 350°F, gas 4) for 1 hour or until a skewer come out clean. Allow the cake to cool before turning it out of the tin and storing in a cake tin. Do not store in an airtight container. This cake will keep for up to one month.

WHOLEWHEAT BANANA AND DATE BREAD
Serves 10

450 g/l lb ripe bananas (about 3 bananas)
225 g/8 oz wholewheat flour
2 teaspoons baking powder
100 g/4 oz soft margarine
75 g/3 oz soft brown sugar
2 eggs, beaten
100 g/4 oz dates, pitted and chopped

Grease and line a 900-g/2-lb loaf tin with greaseproof paper. Peel and mash the bananas. Place the flour and baking powder into a large mixing bowl. Add the margarine, sugar, bananas and eggs and beat with a wooden spoon for 1-2 minutes or just until smooth. Stir in the dates. Spread in the tin and bake in a preheated moderate oven (180°C, 350°F, gas 4) for 1¼ to 1½ hours or until firm. Cool in the tin for 5 minutes before turning out to cool on a wire rack.

DEVON APPLE CAKE

Serves 8 to 10

This moist cake is delicious served warm with Devon clotted cream. It keeps well for up to 1 week or can be frozen.

175 g/6 oz margarine
175 g/6 oz caster sugar
3 eggs, beaten
350 g/12 oz self raising, white or wholewheat flour
225 g/8 oz mixed dried fruit
3 teaspoons mixed spice
450 g/l lb cooking apples, peeled, cored and roughly chopped
3 tablespoons milk

Grease and line a 20-cm/8-inch square cake tin. Cream the margarine and sugar together until light and fluffy. Gradually beat in the eggs adding a little flour if the mixture begins to curdle. Carefully fold in the flour, fruit and spice, until well mixed. Add the apple with enough milk to give a soft mixture. Place the mixture in the cake tin and level the top using the back of a spoon. Bake in a preheated moderate oven (180°C, 350°F, gas 4) for about 1 hour or until firm and golden. Serve warm or cold.

PASSION CAKE
Makes one 22-cm/8½-inch round cake

Don't be put off by the carrots in this cake. They add sweetness, moisture and colour.

175 ml/6 fl oz corn oil
175 g/6 oz caster sugar
3 eggs, size 3
1 teaspoon vanilla essence
100 g/4 oz walnuts, chopped
225 g/8 oz carrots, peeled and grated
175 g/6 oz plain flour
1 teaspoon bicarbonate of soda
1 teaspoon baking powder
1 teaspoon ground cinnamon
1 teaspoon salt

frosting
75 g/3 oz full-fat soft cheese
50 g/2 oz butter, softened
½ teaspoon vanilla essence
100 g/4 oz icing sugar
14 walnut halves

Grease a 22-cm/8½-inch round cake tin and line the base with greased greaseproof paper. Beat together the corn oil, sugar, eggs and vanilla essence. Add the walnuts, grated carrot, flour, bicarbonate of soda, baking powder, cinnamon and salt. Mix well. Pour the mixture into the prepared tin. Bake in a preheated moderate oven (180°C, 350°F, gas 4) for about 1¼ hours until the cake feels firm to the touch. Leave the tin to cool for 5 minutes; then remove the tin and paper and cool on a rack.

To make the frosting, beat together the soft cheese, butter and vanilla essence. Beat in sifted icing sugar until smooth. Spread over the top and sides of the cake and swirl to decorate. Chop 2 walnut halves and sprinkle in the centre of the cake and arrange the remaining walnut halves on the top.

MOIST GUINNESS CAKE
Serves 12 to 15

If you can resist not tasting this cake immediately, store for three to four weeks before eating, to allow it to mature in flavour.

350 g/12 oz butter or margarine
350 g/12 oz soft brown sugar
6 eggs, beaten
425 g/15 oz plain flour
1½ teaspoons ground mixed spice
350 g/12 oz raisins
250 g/9 oz sultanas
175 g/6 oz glaće cherries, quartered
75 g/3 oz mixed peel, chopped
175 g/6 oz walnuts, chopped
finely grated rind of 1 orange
finely grated rind of 1 lemon
225 ml/7½ fl oz Guinness

Cream butter or margarine and sugar until light and fluffy. Gradually beat in eggs. Fold in half the flour and spice with a metal spoon then add all fruit and nuts and finally the remaining flour. Add orange and lemon rinds and half the Guinness. Spoon into a greased and lined 23-cm/9-inch square cake tin. Bake in a preheated moderate oven (160°C, 325°F, gas 3) for 1 hour then reduce to (150°C, 300°F, gas 2) for a further 1½ to 2 hours or until firm to the touch. Allow to cool. When the cake is cold, prick it with a skewer and pour in the remaining Guinness. Wrap in greaseproof paper and store in an airtight tin.

CHOCOLATE ORANGE BUNS
Makes 20

100 g/4 oz butter, softened
75 g/3 oz caster sugar
grated rind of 1 orange
2 eggs, size 3
200 g/7 oz plain flour
2 teaspoons baking powder
pinch of salt
3 tablespoons milk
2 Mars bars

Orange frosting
50 g/2 oz butter, softened
225 g/8 oz icing sugar
2 teaspoons grated orange rind
2 tablespoons orange juice

To make the buns, cream the butter with the sugar and the orange rind until light. Add the eggs, one at a time, beating well after each addition. Sift together the flour, baking powder and salt and stir into the mixture alternately with the milk. Place a small teaspoonful of mixture into 20 paper cake cases. Grate half a Mars bar and reserve for decoration, chop the remainder and divide between the cake cases. Cover with another small teaspoonful of mixture. Bake in a preheated moderate oven (180°C, 350°F, gas 4) for 15–20 minutes until golden and firm to the touch. Cool on a rack.

To make the frosting, beat the butter until smooth. Gradually add the icing sugar, orange rind and juice. Beat until smooth. Spread or pipe a little of the frosting on top of each bun and sprinkle with the reserved grated Mars bar.

STICKY GINGERBREAD
Makes one 18-cm/7-inch square cake

Golden syrup can be used instead of honey if preferred.

4 tablespoons honey
4 tablespoons black treacle
7 tablespoons sunflower oil
100 g/4 oz soft dark brown sugar
150 ml/¼ pint milk
225 g/8 oz Granary flour
½ teaspoon bicarbonate of soda
½ teaspoon salt
3 teaspoons ground ginger
1 egg, size 3

Grease a deep 18-cm/7-inch square cake tin and line the base with greased greaseproof paper. Place the honey, black treacle, sunflower oil, sugar and milk in a saucepan. Heat gently until the sugar has dissolved. Remove from the heat and cool. Sift half the flour into a mixing bowl and reserve the flakes for decoration. Add the remaining flour, bicarbonate of soda, salt and ginger. Make a well in the centre of the flour, add the cooled melted ingredients with the egg and beat until smooth. Pour into the prepared tin, sprinkle the reserved wheat flakes over the top and bake in a preheated cool oven (150°C, 300°F, gas 2) for about 1 hour 20 minutes until well risen and firm to the touch. Leave to cool in the tin for 15 minutes; then loosen the edges with a knife, turn out, remove the paper and cool on a rack. Serve sliced, spread with butter.

PARKIN
Makes 9 squares

Traditionally eaten on Guy Fawkes Night, this good sticky cake from Yorkshire helps keep out the cold while you huddle round the bonfire.

2 teaspoons bicarbonate of soda
150 ml/¼ pint milk
100 g/4 oz lard
100 g/4 oz margarine
75 g/3 oz granulated sugar
100 g/4 oz golden syrup
100 g/4 oz black treacle
225 g/8 oz plain flour
225 g/8 oz medium oatmeal
2 teaspoons ground ginger
1 teaspoon salt

Grease a 20-cm/8-inch square cake tin and line the base with greased greaseproof paper. Dissolve the bicarbonate of soda in the milk. Place the lard, margarine, sugar, golden syrup and black treacle in a saucepan and heat gently until the fats have melted and the sugar dissolved. Remove from the heat and add the remaining ingredients including the milk. Mix until well blended and pour into the prepared tin. Bake in a preheated moderate oven (160°C, 325°F, gas 3) for about 1 hour until dark brown and firm. Leave in the tin to cool; then turn out. It is best stored in a cake tin for 2 days before eating. Serve cut into squares.

BLACK BUN
Serves 12

This Scottish Bun is traditionally served at Hogmanay, but was originally served on Twelfth Night. Make it at least two weeks in advance. It will keep for up to two months in an airtight tin.

for the pastry
350 g/12 oz plain flour
pinch of salt
75 g/3 oz lard
75 g/3 oz margarine

for the filling
450 g/1 lb seedless raisins
450 g/1 lb currants
50 g/2 oz chopped almonds
50 g/2 oz chopped mixed peel
175 g/6 oz plain flour
75 g/3 oz soft brown sugar
1 teaspoon ground allspice
½ teaspoon ground ginger
½ teaspoon ground cinnamon
½ teaspoon baking powder
2 tablespoons brandy
1 large egg
3 tablespoons milk

To make the pastry sift the flour and salt into a large bowl, add the lard and margarine, and rub in with the fingertips until the mixture resembles fine breadcrumbs. Add sufficient cold water to bind to a soft dough. Chill. Then roll two-thirds of the pastry out and use to line the base and sides of a 450-g/1-lb loaf tin.

To make the filling mix all the ingredients together to give a solid firm dropping consistency. The mixture should not be wet. Pack the fruit mixture firmly into the pastry case. Roll out the remaining pastry to make the lid. Dampen and seal the edges well. Using a skewer, make 4 holes right through the bun, then prick the top with a fork.

Bake in a preheated moderate oven (160°C, 325°F, gas 3) for 3 hours. Allow to cool completely before storing in a tin. Do not store in an airtight plastic container.

TRADITIONAL SCOTTISH SHORTBREAD

Makes 8 wedges

The addition of semolina gives extra crispness and a melt-in-the-mouth texture. For added crunch and flavour, sprinkle chopped hazelnuts over the shortbread before baking.

50 g/2 oz caster sugar
100 g/4 oz unsalted butter, softened
150 g/5 oz plain flour
25 g/1 oz fine semolina
caster sugar, for dredging

Cream together the sugar and butter until pale, light and fluffy. Stir in the flour and semolina, using a fork. Press the mixture into an 18-cm/7-inch round sandwich tin. Smooth the surface using a palette knife and decorate the edges using a fork. Prick all over with a fork and sprinkle with caster sugar. Bake in a preheated moderate oven (160°C, 325°F, gas 3) for about 1 hour. The shortbread should be pale but just beginning to colour. Cool in the tin for 15 minutes; then mark into 8 wedges. Carefully ease out of the tin and cool on a wire rack. Store in an airtight container.

CHOCOLATE COCONUT CRUNCH

Makes nine squares

Chocolate glacé icing instead of melted chocolate can be spread over the biscuits.

115 g/4½ oz plain flour
25 g/1 oz cocoa powder
15 g/½ oz desiccated coconut
50 g/2 oz caster sugar
100 g/4 oz butter
25 g/1 oz milk chocolate

Sift the flour and cocoa into a bowl. Stir in the coconut and caster sugar. Rub in the butter until the mixture sticks together and forms a firm dough. Press the dough into an 18-cm/7-inch square shallow tin and smooth the surface. Prick all over with a fork. Bake in a preheated moderate oven (160°C, 325°F, gas 3) for 1 hour. Cool in the tin.

Cut into nine squares and carefully ease out of the tin. Melt the chocolate in a small bowl over a pan of hot, but not boiling, water. Place in a small piping bag with a plain writing nozzle and drizzle chocolate over the top; alternatively, drizzle the chocolate from a teaspoon.

LEMON SPICE SHORTBREAD

Makes about 22 biscuits

Grated clementine, satsuma or orange rind makes a good alternative to lemon rind.

175 g/6 oz plain flour
½ teaspoon ground cinnamon
pinch of salt
1 teaspoon finely grated lemon rind
50 g/ 2 oz caster sugar
100 g/4 oz butter

Sift together the flour, cinnamon and salt. Stir in the lemon rind and sugar. Rub in the butter until the mixture clings together. Roll out the dough to 5-mm/¼-inch thickness and cut into fingers 2.5 × 7.5 cm/1 × 3 inches. Transfer to a greased baking tray. Prick neatly with a fork and bake in a preheated moderate oven (160°C, 325°F, gas 3) for 15-20 minutes. Cool on a wire rack and dredge with caster sugar. Store in an airtight container.

WHOLEMEAL DATE SHORTBREAD

Makes 8 wedges

Half wholemeal and half white flour can be used if preferred.

150 g/5 oz wholemeal flour
25 g/1 oz cornflour
50 g/2 oz light soft brown sugar
100 g/4 oz butter
50 g/2 oz dates, chopped
2 teaspoons demerara sugar (optional)

Mix together the wholemeal flour, cornflour and sugar in a mixing bowl. Rub in the butter until the mixture forms a dough; then work in the dates. Place on a baking tray and form the dough into a round about 1 cm/½ inch thick. Mark into eight segments and prick with a fork. Flute the edges. Bake in a preheated moderate oven (160°C, 325°F, gas 3) for about 35 minutes until firm. Cool on a rack and sprinkle with demerara sugar.

LEMON CARAWAY CAKE
Makes 6 to 8 slices

Tangy and light, this cake is not too sweet. Ask the family to guess the flavour!

175 g/6 oz butter or margarine
175 g/6 oz soft brown sugar
rind and juice of 1 lemon
3 eggs, separated
250 g/9 oz self raising wholemeal flour
2 teaspoons caraway seeds

icing
100 g/4 oz low-fat soft cheese
2 tablespoons icing sugar
1 tablespoon lemon juice

Cream the butter or margarine and sugar together until light and fluffy. Add the finely grated lemon rind. Gradually beat in the egg yolks; then stir in the flour, caraway seeds and lemon juice. Stiffly whisk the egg whites and fold into the cake mixture, using a large metal spoon. Turn the mixture into a greased and lined 18-cm/7-inch round cake tin and bake in a preheated moderate oven (180°C, 350°F, gas 4) for 1 hour. Turn onto a wire rack to cool.

To make icing, beat the soft cheese with the sugar and lemon juice and spread over the top of the cake.

PECAN BROWNIES
12 brownies

Moist and chewy, an American favourite! Use walnuts instead of Pecans if you prefer.

225 g/8 oz margarine
375 g/13 oz caster sugar
1½ teaspoons vanilla essence
4 size 3 eggs
100 g/4 oz plain flour
75 g/3 oz cocoa powder
½ teaspoon baking powder
½ teaspoon salt
100 g/4 oz pecan nuts, roughly chopped

Icing:
100 g/4 oz plain chocolate, grated
50 g/2 oz butter
1 egg, beaten
175 g/6 oz icing sugar, sifted
12 pecan nuts

Grease, and line the base of a 28 × 18 × 2.5-cm/11 × 7 × 1-inch tin. Melt the margarine and pour it into a large bowl. Add the sugar and vanilla essence. Add the eggs one at a time, beating well after each addition. Sift the flour, cocoa, baking powder and salt and add them to the mixture. Mix well and stir in the nuts. Transfer the mixture to the tin.

Bake in the centre of a moderate oven (180°C, 350°F, gas 4) for 40 minutes. Leave the cake in the tin to cool completely.

To ice:

Melt the chocolate with the butter in a bowl over a saucepan of hot water. Stir in the eggs and remove the bowl from the heat. Gradually beat in the icing sugar until the mixture is smooth. Allow it to cool until the frosting is thick enough to stand in soft peaks. Spread or swirl it over the cake, decorate with pecans, and cut into 12 squares and leave to set.

ALMOND SLICES
Makes 18 slices

175 g/6 oz plain flour
pinch of salt
75 g/3 oz margarine
6 tablespoons raspberry jam
2 egg whites
100 g/4 oz ground almonds
50 g/2 oz ground rice
150 g/6 oz caster sugar
4 tablespoons cold water
50 g/2 oz flaked almonds

Sift the flour and salt into a large bowl. Add the margarine and rub in with the fingertips until the mixture resembles breadcrumbs. Stir in enough cold water to give a soft dough. Roll out the pastry on a lightly floured work surface to fit a 30 × 18-cm/12 × 8-inch oblong Swiss roll tin. Trim the edges and spread the jam over the pastry. Lightly beat the egg whites with a fork and add the ground almonds, rice, sugar and water. Spread this almond paste over the jam and sprinkle with the flaked almonds. Bake in a preheated moderately hot oven (190°C, 375°F, gas 5) for 30 to 35 minutes until golden. Allow to cool; then cut into slices.

MACAROONS
Makes 18 biscuits

These are delicious served with creamy fruit desserts or hot trifles.

2 egg whites
100 g/4 oz ground almonds
225 g/8 oz caster sugar
15 g/½ oz ground rice
½ teaspoon vanilla essence
½ teaspoon almond essence
18 blanched almonds

Line 2 baking trays with silicone kitchen paper or rice paper. Whisk the egg whites until they form soft peaks. Fold in the almonds, sugar, rice and essences. Mix well. Spoon 18 mounds of mixture, well apart, onto the lined trays. Press a blanched almond onto the middle of each mound. Bake in a preheated moderate oven (160°C, 325°F, gas 3) for 25 minutes, or until the biscuits are pale gold in colour. Allow the biscuits to stand for 5 minutes before lifting them off the trays. (If using rice paper, carefully trim this around the edges of the biscuits). Cool the bisuits completely on a wire cooling rack.

ALMOND CURLS
Makes 24 biscuits

These attractive biscuits are delicious with hot fruit salads or any creamy dessert.

75 g/3 oz butter
75 g/3 oz caster sugar
50 g/2 oz plain flour
75 g/3 oz flaked almonds

Cream the butter and sugar together in a mixing bowl, until they are pale and fluffy. Stir in the flour and the almonds. Line 2 baking sheets with silicone kitchen paper. Spoon 24 mounds of the biscuit mixture onto the baking sheets, allowing plenty of space for the mixture to spread. Flatten the mounds gently with the back of a damp fork. Bake in a preheated moderately hot oven (200°C, 400°F, gas 6) for 6-8 minutes, or until the biscuits are pale gold.

Allow the biscuits to stand for 1 minute, then remove them from the baking sheets with a palette knife. Place each biscuit onto a rolling pin and carefully press it around the upper half to curl. Leave the biscuits to set and then remove them very carefully.

Note: If the biscuits begin to harden on the baking sheets, pop them back into the oven for about 1 minute, so that they become pliable again.

SPONGE FINGERS
Makes 20 biscuits

Speed is of the essence when preparing these biscuits, as the light fluffy mixture will lose its volume if it is allowed to stand for too long.

50 g/2 oz caster sugar
2 eggs
2-3 drops of vanilla essence
50 g/2 oz plain flour
caster sugar, for dredging

Line 2 baking sheets with silicone kitchen paper. Beat the sugar, eggs and vanilla essence together in a bowl, using a rotary or electric whisk, until the mixture is pale and creamy. Quickly and gently, fold in the flour. Fit a piping bag with a 1-cm/½-inch plain nozzle and use this to pipe finger lengths of the sponge mixture onto the baking sheets, allowing plenty of space between each biscuit as the mixture will spread. Dredge the sponges liberally with caster sugar and bake in a preheated moderately hot oven (190°C, 375°F, gas 5) for 6-8 minutes, or until the biscuits are light golden brown. Cool the biscuits completely on a wire rack.

INDEX